GW00566964

PROUD SEAS AND CORNWALL'S PAST

PROUD SEAS
AND
CORNWALL'S PAST

NIGEL TANGYE

WILLIAM KIMBER · LONDON

First published in 1982 by
WILLIAM KIMBER & CO. LIMITED
Godolphin House, 22a Queen Anne's Gate,
London, SW1H 9AE

© Nigel Tangye, 1982
ISBN 0-7183-0079-3

Photoset by Keystroke Limited, Godalming
and printed in Great Britain by
Biddles Limited, Guildford and King's Lynn

Contents

*A map of Spray's voyage
appears on pages 48–49*

Acknowledgements

For their help in providing me with research material, I offer my sincere thanks to the following: Miss Joan Bailey, Deputy Assistant Librarian of the London Library; to Miss Angela Broome, Assistant Librarian, the Royal Institution of Cornwall; to Mr G. T. Knight, County Local Studies Librarian; to Mr E. Needham, Senior Librarian, Cornwall County Library; and to Mr J. Stephens, Librarian of Newquay County Library.

Finally, I would like to thank the Curator of Truro Museum, Mr H. L. Douch, for his willingness always to share the fruits of his scholarship with lesser mortals; and to thank the Assistant Curator, Mr R. D. Penhallurick, for creating for me his delightful map.

NIGEL TANGYE
Glendorgal Lodge, April 1982

By Way of a Preface

I hope, in this book, to provide the reader with an enjoyable few hours as we share together an informal survey of memorable lives and events in the story of Cornwall.

In the writing of it I have had in the front of my mind that ever-growing number of people who are interested in Cornwall, who have a 'thing' for Cornwall (may the purist forgive me) but who do not feel equipped enough to delve into conventional history books. Hopefully, I may help to expand the horizon of those of us who are more and more seeking, unconsciously, assurance from archaeology, historical records, artefacts, biographies, even vintage car clubs or old picture postcards, as a counter to our anxiety regarding the future and the onrush of technology. The worldwide membership of the Cornwall Family History Society speaks for itself.

I believe that this groping into the past by ordinary people who would by no stretch of the imagination see themselves as historians is encouraged by the comfort of being persuaded that each of us is a particle in the ever-moving stream of history whose momentum drives through the present and into the future. This identification as fellow-human beings with those in past generations, men and women with ills and joys and foibles like ourselves, gives us a satisfying sense of belonging, which itself brings its own brand of security.

This sense of belonging is vividly felt by anyone who, never having looked further back than his grandparents, suddenly finds through some modest research that he is of a proven line going back several generations. From then on he feels a bigger, more confident individual.

And so it is that in pursuit of the foregoing, these people whom I withdraw from their historic environment of time and space, those characters who have provided the weft and the warp of the Cornish tapestry, I present to my readers who might otherwise not meet them.

To effect this, I invite the reader on board my sailing ketch, *Spray,* to share my experience as she cruises around the coast of Cornwall. In three previous books – *Voyage into Cornwall's Past, The Living Breath of Cornwall* and *Cornwall and the Tumbling Sea* – we have sailed through time and over sea from Hartland Point down to Land's End, to the Scilly Islands, and along the south coast as far as Helford.

There is a saying that the sea is an obstacle to be overcome, and is not a blessing like the earth. The Cornish would claim this only partly true, but it signifies a reason for the Cornish character. The miner, 2,000 feet underground, and the seamen roaming the uncharted oceans, have set the rest the example of taking things as they come, always ready for the worst that the elements can throw at them.

But for us, we who seek to light up the path and environment of history, the sea has a very special feature to offer us. To the onlooker the sea looks today precisely the same as it looked ten thousand, a million years ago.

The sea is unique. Time brings with it erosion and decay, not permitting me to share with past generations the precise visual experience of seeing what they saw.

Not so the sea. The sea is unchanging, it responds to wind and weather as it always has throughout time. The seaman today views it as did the seaman of yesterday, and as did the first of our race in times of pre-history.

And no one has more reason to know the sea better than the Celtic race, the Cornish, who predominate in this strange proboscis of England that thrusts itself out into the Atlantic Ocean, its back turned on what the British used to call until recently the Mother Country.

From here, from this small area of sea-girt, windswept land, has been raised a breed of man that has played through time roles of remarkable distinction by any standards, in the highest factions of realm and government, of learning, of science, of mining, of engineering, of worldwide trade and exploration overseas, of naval prowess.

Wandering through Cornwall, the enquiring visitor will see evidence of this propensity to lead and initiate. It goes back to pre-history. Nowhere is there a more exciting place than Cornwall for this revelation, this union with our forebears, than here.

From my window, without my moving a yard, I can see the marks left by men who dwelt in my area through thousands of preceding centuries.

From here I look across Porth Bay to Trevelgue Island, which was a cliff castle two to three thousand years ago with five lines of defence on which you can pick up items of Iron Age or Stone Age man's refuse at any time. The bay, open-ended to the Atlantic, nevertheless was a commercial haven for boats on the coastal trade until early this century.

Recalling, as I do, black-tarred smacks with grubby sails delivering coal from Wales to this exposed haven, there rips across the sky before my eyes a jet plane from St Mawgan aerodrome three miles away and which is included in the view for me with two Bronze Age burial tombs on the tip of Whipsiderry cliff. And there's a third and a fourth over there to the left, and an Iron Age mine-working just below.

And then, my vision leaps over these early ages to embrace the Victorian; for seven miles or so up the coastline of high cliffs, the diminishing perspective leads me to the promontory on which was built the first North Coast Lighthouse, a light which represents one of the first major navigational advances in the art of safeguarding shipping, and developed by a Cornishman, Goldsworthy Gurney.

As I write the foregoing I realise to my astonishment that though I am familiar with each and every facet of those individual representations of different periods I have never thought of them wedded together in the same context, of the panorama of time and human existence they represent in the

Cornish story. But now the wonder of this line of continuity on my 'patch' is there to stay with me.

The Cornishman, perhaps fortified by his Celtic blood and these many differing monuments around him, tends to take the wonder of Cornwall for granted. And what do I mean by 'wonder'? Surely it is something spiritual that is invested in something material, and which stimulates the imagination to embrace it with wonder.

In the following pages I invite the reader to share with me the wonder that persists throughout the telling of the story of Cornwall.

Sometimes, it may be thought while we are sharing the company of those individuals I have chosen to introduce you to, that we may seem to depart somewhat from their Cornish base. This I would not agree with, for in considering the nature of one man's life there is brought to one's attention the shape of day to day life, of period manners, compared with what we experience today. Cornwall will always be the predominant feature on which the story is based.

I counsel the reader to draw from the foregoing a conception of how life in vastly differing spheres, emanating from Cornwall, differed in the living of it. The biography of a man is a vehicle for feeling this.

I

Setting the Scene

'One afternoon in early summer I was visiting the strange complex of spectacular jumbled rock and vegetation of Hartland Point. Hither, the tough, arrogant Cornish coast strides up from Land's End...'

The foregoing will ring a bell in the minds of readers who have shared with me the previous sections of our cruise round the Cornish Coast, evoking, from the scene we pass, the human side of the story of Cornwall.

To them I ask forbearance while I re-establish, for the sake of new readers of this book, the circumstances from which the pattern of the telling of it was born. It will only take a couple of pages, no offence will be taken by this author if anyone skips them!

*

While I was standing on the cliff edge at Hartland Point, just beyond the county boundary, on that summer's day, the idea of viewing the history of my county came to me.

Far down below, the sea was lazily running up and along a plateau of serrated rock whose murderously savage character even the placid incoming swell could not conceal.

The rock was formed in narrow, parallel ribs, as individual in their fashioning as the venerable pillar rocks of Land's End. Seaward, beyond the smooth expanse of calm sea looking to me precisely the same as it looked to the onlooker ten thousand years ago, ten million years perhaps, lay the horizon, not a sharp line on this afternoon but a soft finale to the smooth blue sea.

I ponder on the strange property of the sea that gives it a unique quality in terms of time. I look at the cliffs stretching north and southward, and at the landscape behind me and, as I have already said in a different context, I know that time leaves erosion and decay, altering the face of the earth and man's artefacts upon it, so that I am not permitted by nature to share with past generations, precisely, the visual experience of seeing what they saw.

Not so with the sea. The sea is unchanging. The winds may ruffle it, rumple it, torment it, but the sea responds in exactly the same way as it always has. The seaman today views it as did the seaman of yesterday, and as did the first of our race in times of pre-recorded history.

Dwelling on this immensely exciting thought, that there is such a visual link spanning the ages, between ourselves and primitive man and all the generations between, I looked down from my cliff top, and my attention was back in the present; for, far down below and slowly approaching from the north on the silent blue sea was a white yacht, like a resting seabird.

She was sailing southward, and she had her spinnaker up, rotund and white like the breast of a well-fed, satiated gull on the water, smoothly paddling. With wind astern she glided slowly along her path, a divine picture of contentment, a boat in her element on a lovely day.

I wondered if those on board this leisure craft would do more than glance at the phalanx of cliffs on this calm day, and if they would see in their geological face the character of Cornwall, from the rugged stubbornness of rock defying the assault of wind and sea to the kindliness of pasture and flowers in the winding combes that shape the path of stream to ocean. And I wondered if those on board felt the presence of their fellow seamen in storm and tempest in these waters over the centuries, their spirits lingering in the countless tangled wrecks that line the cliff foot from Hartland Point to Land's End.

The white yacht had no fears. She was by now but a calm speck on the limpid sea, and I envied those on board cruising down this historic coast so serenely, with the opportunity presented them to sense, or to read, or to ponder as they passed, the history inland from the great cliff; from beyond the sand-washed estuary and within the unsheltered bay.

It was two years later that I found myself in my ketch, *Spray*, turning south off Hartland Point, following in the wake of the white seabird, and receptive to the voice of Cornwall in the cry of the gulls, the swish of spray, and thunder of tumbling waves.

Cruising down the north coast in *Spray*, as I then was, I allowed my thoughts to wander. Sometimes, the great cliffs, or the yellow beach, sent a message to me, a call to the past, and I would wonder what circumstance, what event in the past might be the trigger that set my mind turning with the revolving wheel of history.

Soon, I would relate, quite clearly, to someone or something that had a clue planted for me amongst the serried surfaces of those legendary, loquacious cliffs.

Spray has carried us, as related in my afore-mentioned books, right down the north coast to Land's End, across to the Scilly Islands, back into Mount's Bay and then around the Lizard past the Manacles rocks to where she lies now, to where we are going to join her, to complete the cruise through history along the south coast and into Plymouth Sound, the western side of which is Cornish.

Spray is waiting for us at her mooring in the Helford river just off the Helford village steps. It is some weeks since I left her there in company with the shade of *Sunbeam*, the pre-war schooner which served as the headquarters vessel of the secret operations unit from whence, for a great part of the war, secret agents were sent across the Channel to and fro on their dangerous missions to France and the French Resistance forces. This story is told in my book *Cornwall and the Tumbling Sea*.

Now, have a good look with me on this sunny June morning at *Spray*, as a dinghy takes us out to her mooring. She is 30 feet long, two-masted, and ketch-rigged, with varnished hull glistening in the sun as we approach. Her coach roof is light blue.

Stepping down into her cockpit we find protection from the elements either side in the form of a gleaming white canvas wind-break made fast to the steel stanchions of the guard rails.

I get a thrill every time I board my boat. Memories of stormy nights together, of placid dawns, fill my mind. As does the picture of one of her class (*Falmouth Pilot* designed by Nigel Warington-Smyth) at sea showing off her beauty, beguiling me into being her slave sometime, somehow.

I was sailing another boat when I first saw one of this Pilot Class. She was sailing full and bye out of Falmouth. She was ahead, crossing my bow, this beautiful boat, heeling to the wind, the sun glinting on her wet hull, she gliding over the dappled golden sea which was flecked with a thousand wavelet shadows. As she slid over this golden carpet, her sails leaning to the breeze, her bow lifting to the lively waves, I fell head over heels in love with her.

I fell in love with her sensuality, present in the make-up of all boats but abundant in this lovely thing, which I knew I was going to have to possess; the curve of her hull glistening, smooth, wet, exposed momentarily to view as a gust presses on her, the shape of her wind-filled sail, full and quivering a little, the thrust of her mainmast stretching upwards to the sky, her brave stern cleaving the living water; parted, shining white teeth of the bow wave and the coquettish trickle of her wake, spent, astern, lifting, sinking, lifting and sinking to the rounded rhythm of the sea, slaps of water and splashes against the curved expanse of her hull, and the caress of the breeze as one stands poised, alone with her, standing at her stem, hand on stay, she thrusting through the submissive sea: yes, already I felt her tiller in my hand, the favours she would bestow on him who pleases, and her fury if I were to mishandle her.

And now, let us be away on the first stage of our passage eastward along the south coast, receptive to the voice of Cornwall through the ages, in the sound of the gulls, the pulsing swish of spray.

I will allow my thoughts to wander. Sometimes a massive cliff, or a yellow beach will send a message to me, a call to the past; or the sight of a vessel emerging from a fishing port will cause me to wonder what circumstance, what event had set my mind turning with the revolving wheel of history.

And then I will relate, quite clearly, to someone or something that had a clue for me planted amongst the serried surfaces of those legendary, loquacious, slopes and cliffs.

Yes, the time has come for me to slip the mooring, take advantage of the ebbing tide out of the mouth of the Helford River, and steer into what our passage has in store for us.

II

The Fal, Black Rock, and the Sea

I do not have long to wait before, a mile or so out into Falmouth Bay, I feel enveloped by the aura of past ships and seamen setting off on long voyages of exploration; of Post Office packets returning to their home port with mail and bullion from their 90-day round trip to the merchants of the West Indies; of naval frigates and transports sailing supplies and replacements to Corunna and Lisbon in the Peninsular War.

This empty sea, Falmouth Bay, that *Spray* is passing through now, teems with nautical shadows, of shades of vessels from afar on the last lap of voyages from distant parts, of naval vessels. For Falmouth, until the coming of steam vessels early in the first half of the last century, was a major port for the overseas business of commercial activities – London merchants chief among them.

As it took the coach four days to get to London, and a goods waggon at least eleven, this may seem surprising. Was not London, itself, you may ask, an important port? Yes, it certainly was – but sometimes it could take a vessel as much as *ten weeks* to beat westward up the Channel in contrary winds, arriving at Falmouth for replenishment when she should be at her journey's end.

Falmouth is a marvellous natural harbour and we shall be enjoying aspects of this in due course. For now I want to relate an alarming experience of the kind which engenders the aura of drama to which I have already referred.

Spray is taking us through the bay for a call at Falmouth. She ripples along in the smooth water, her sails comfortably relaxed with only a gentle breeze pressing just hard enough to create a curve in them. I take the opportunity to recall the remarkable experience that faced the inhabitants of this potential prize for the King's enemies.

One day in August 1779 the inhabitants were alarmed to waken and find the bay full of ships. All on shore were alarmed for they had never seen before anything so spectacular, so mysterious in its silent presence, as this enemy fleet that filled the bay: for it *was* the enemy. It was the French fleet and we were at war with France.

The town held its breath expecting anything to happen. Instead, the day passed peacefully enough, except for that frightening presence of a huge arsenal of power that remained apparently languidly in the bay.

On the following day all had returned to normal. Joshua Fox, a shipping agent, of Tregedna, sat down and wrote a letter, telling of the eventful day, to his brother:

You will no doubt be most surprised when I tell you the consternation we were all thrown into last night by the appearance of the French fleet off this Place, and some of their Frigates so near as three miles off Castlehead [Pendennis].

At about 6 a.m. we first discovered them from the Hill as Mr Bell and myself were looking at three Ships going, as we imagined, to join the Fleet and really were so, but they could not get past as the enemy extended almost across the Channel. The *Marlborough, Iris* and *Southampton* were the ships going to join Sir Charles Hardy, and the *Iris* had a narrow escape from being taken.

About ten o'clock an officer from the *Southampton* came here with a confirmation of what they were, of which I was well assured the moment I discovered them with my glass, and to proceed immediately to Penzance to get a vessel to carry a Despatch to an Admiral who was cruising from ten to twenty leagues off Scilly. Plane has gone from hence in an open Shallop, and as we have heard of his passing the Lizard am in hopes he will reach the Fleet tonight, the wind being

Southerly, how they could have got here without our Fleet seeing them is astonishing.

You will expect I should say something about their Number and Force to neither of which I can assert positively except that the Officer of the *Southampton* told me he counted from the Mizen top-mast head *seventy-six* sail [!] and from the number of small vessels which I could see with my glass which consisted of about 26 sail, and therefore I think I may venture to say they do not consist of less than *fifty sail of the line* which God knows is enough.

And here we are now, in *Spray*, right where the middle of this formidable force hovered, that night 200 years ago.

Looking around him, marking the coastline of the bay in which his fleet containing some 20,000 men or more was enclosed, the Admiral would see its contours and the hills just as we see them today; and beneath *Spray's* keel no doubt an immersed archaeologist would find throwaway containers serving the same purpose as bottles and cans do today. Certainly, the feel and the look of the water which has not changed feeds one's imagination in a way that causes two centuries of time to disappear.

In his letter at this point, Mr Fox provides an interesting spotlight on the kind of naval force of ours that was based in Falmouth. 'I flatter myself we shall be a match for them,' he writes, 'as we have such a number of Capital Ships, altogether 38 sail of the Line, to Frigates, Fire-ships, etc., etc.' He goes on:

> The enemy now extend from the Manacles to the Deadman's Point, and I now see eleven large ships from the Hill. Their intentions cannot be discovered. The *Grantham* Packet is put back.

Their intentions never were discovered, for the French fleet left in as mysterious a fashion as it had arrived.

The calm tone of Mr Fox's letter surely conceals what must have been a frighteningly confused twenty-four hours for the

people of Falmouth, this menace hanging over them, their
ignorance of what could befall them, their fears of what could
happen.

Six months later, Joshua Fox was writing to his brother in
happier circumstances:

> The East India Fleet consisting of two ships and a Frigate,
> with two fleets from the West Indies, as well as one from
> Oporto bound home, are all come into our Port except a few
> from the Leonard Islands which are gone up the Channel.
>
> Our harbour looks quite cheerful with about 200 sail of
> Vessels in sight from our house. They have lost but one
> Vessel which was a Transport sunk in a storm, most of the
> Men were saved, the fleet are very valuable, the town is full of
> Passengers from the fleets. Plane took a small Privateer
> which was between the fleet and our Castle, they were so
> near that we could hear the Gun from our Parlour.

A little later in the same year Joshua tells his brother of another
event to celebrate: but here I would like to interpolate a
message to the reader, and commend him to picture the scenes
described in these letters and to remember that all this took
place off the same Falmouth we know today, in the same setting
where white yachts lazily cruise about.

This further letter has the dateline August 1780, and he
writes that

> On Thursday, the *Flora* Frigate of 40 guns brought in the
> *Nymph* French Frigate of 36 guns, which she took after a stout
> resistance of near two hours, they fought some time within
> Pistol shot, but the latter part of the engagement they were so
> near that they could not fire the great Guns, but were obliged
> to use small arms and Pikes, the French lost her Captain, two
> Lieutenants and forty others killed and a number wounded,
> in all supposed to be about 120.
>
> Ours lost about 10 killed, and about 18 wounded, among
> the killed were Midshipmen. The French vessel is exceed-

ingly shattered, one shot carried off all the Muzzle of one of
their Guns, others (went) through their decks, but one
Lieutenant and one Midshipman unhurt out of all the
Officers.

She is a very fine Vessel. No other news. The Grand Fleet
passed by the Harbour for Spithead last evening. Thee must
excuse a short letter as it's late, and I am obliged to dress to
drink tea with the Ambassador at his lodgings.

And I in *Spray*, on this summer afternoon, glide over these
waters that have borne so much grandeur, sensed so many joys,
witnessed the fears and excitements of so many seafarers.

Can it be right, is it seemly, that I and humble *Spray* should
share the elements with such grand events? Perhaps. I reflect
that together with the great who have passed before us we share
a common respect, facing the same demands made on our skill
by tide and current and wind. Above all, we know together the
spectre of the lurking alchemy of storm and gale and violent
seas.

As a matter of fact, it must have been in the area *Spray* is in
now, approaching the entrance to Falmouth just a mile away,
that one of the most famous figures in history kept his mind
wistfully fixed on what might have been, as he viewed the
entrance to Falmouth harbour as one of the final stages – a very
muted one – of his dramatic life was played out; but it was out of
his reach. Napoleon Buonaparte was being transferred from
the *Bellerophon* to the *Northumberland* on his way, after his defeat
at Waterloo, to exile in St Helena.

The *Bellerophon*, Captain Maitland, to whom Napoleon had
surrendered, had been in Plymouth Sound for some days
attracting much attention to the delight of the local boatmen
from Cawsand and elsewhere. On 5th August 1815 the *Royal
Cornwall Gazette* reported:

The *Bellerophon* has been surrounded by boats, all swarming
with curious folk from all parts of the country, anxious to get

a glimpse of *emperor rasee* [sic], and a variety of accounts have
been published in newspapers from those *fearless* and
intelligent voyagers: who all concur in assuring us that
Buonaparte wears a green coat, and generally walks with his
hands behind his back! Their other information is equally
interesting.

At the same time as we are willing to hope that most of
those persons who have been so anxious to 'see Buonaparte'
are actuated by views that are *simply innocent*! We cannot help
remarking, on the other hand, how much his vanity is
sheltered, his disgrace softened, and his sense of guilt
removed, by those demonstrations which certainly savour
none of that neglect and contempt with which such a being
ought to be treated.

Shakespeare has a speech so pertinent to this occasion that
we cannot refuse ourselves the pleasure of quoting it:

'A strange fish! Were I in England now, and had but this
fish painted, not a holiday fool there but would give a piece of
silver: there would this monster make a man – any strange
beast there makes a man!'

The *Gazette*, elsewhere in the same edition, expressed editorial
disgust, beyond endurance, on learning of the respect with
which the ruffian had been treated on board the *Bellerophon*
'where British officers have been forced to walk bare-headed
before the detested murderer... can degradation descend
lower?'

The reception given by the public from the fleet of small
boats has within its framework an element of what might have
been *déja vu* if, a century or so later it had been Hitler in
Plymouth Sound surrounded by little boats with gaping awe-
struck sightseers.

The *Royal Cornwall Gazette* informed the public, with just
dismay that 'a considerable number of people in boats', standing off the *Bellerophon*, '*took off their hats and cheered the tyrant*'. It
goes on to lament that this should have happened in Plymouth
Sound, 'a place whose shores had never echoed to any other

shouts than those of loyalty and patriotic exaltation'.

In the middle of the entrance to the capacious harbour of Falmouth, between the arms of St Anthony and Pendennis is the Black Rock, which has the rare virtue of being potentially a dangerous obstacle to incoming vessels, covered and not visible at flood tide, yet blessed with the relief of countless mariners through history who, once past Black Rock, after long, stormy passages, know that they have at last reached shelter.

In *Spray*, I always carry with me a copy of the 1859 *Channel Pilot*, of which more anon, it being a means of truly looking over the shoulder of a navigator under sail as he makes his passage and brings his vessel into Falmouth a hundred or so years ago.

Let me quote a few lines from this to give the reader a taste of the flavour of entering the haven:

> Nearly in the middle of the entrance, and almost opposite Pendennis Castle lies a rock called *Falmouth*, or *Black Rock*: it appears at half-tide, and has a stone beacon upon it to show where it lies when overflowed by the tide. You may go on either side of the *Black Rock*; but the eastern side is the best, where you will have from 6 to 16 fathoms of water.
>
> The channel to the westward of the rock is both narrower and shoaler... but when Black Rock is covered, there is sufficient water for the largest ships.
>
> ... In all westerly winds, but particularly in the summer season, ships of the line and men-of-war in general, having occasion to call at this port for supplies, will find it more convenient to anchor without the points of Pendennis and St Anthony than to entangle themselves with the interior anchorage of Carrick Road ...

I like that word 'entangled'. It provides a vivid picture of the anchorage in the Carrick Roads when as many as two hundred sailing vessels of all kinds might be anchored there at one time.

We are not yet in the Roads, not yet past Black Rock, but now I can see it quite clearly. Indeed, it has been in view a long time but *Spray*, her sails trying to attract a wind that has died away to nothing, and her hull heading into an ebbing tide, has meant we have made no headway for some half hour. How fortunate that the enemy fleet is not still in the Bay or we would be gobbled up never to be seen again!

However, even without a ghost fleet to hem her in it seems it will be late before we get into harbour. Not that it matters, for *Spray* and I have nothing to do but keep each other company and in touch with the reader.

Nothing to do? Perhaps not, but my mind is working over-time, for the magic of the sea as a time dissipater is working again, and the years, centuries, are slipping away so that I am alive to a new force, another aspect of the value of Cornwall in world, history-making affairs. And this feature that I now have in mind was witnessed by this same Black Rock that we are slowly approaching, this rock which great and little ships have passed on their lawful, and unlawful, occasions, maybe their captains either bracing themselves for a long voyage or thanking God for delivery at last from a hazardous one.

As things turn out we enter the Roads before dark, and this rather saddens me for I love the sense of wonder a seaman gets at night at sea – all the more so in such a stretch of water as this. I wholly identify myself with all the seamen who have preceded me in these waters.

To be alone at sea in a boat at night is as if you were on a bridge that spans time, or rather defuses it so that the experience is precisely the same as it was for those in ages past.

The reason for this is that nothing has changed, as I have already mentioned, but, more positively, there is the experience, heightened at night at sea, of the unchanged message to eye and ear, the dark velvet of night and the glow of starlight on the restless water, the haphazard splashes of water against the hull, the soft zephyrs of air upon the cheek.

All this I share with the seamen of the ages. From it I draw, like they did, the warmth of community and comradeship; and the humility from being in what is surely the presence of God.

We pass Black Rock in full light. We can pass with plenty of water either side, but let us see again what the century old *Channel Pilot* advises as being the better with the sailing vessel in mind.

> You may go on either side of Black Rock, but the eastern side is the better, where you will have from 6 to 16 fathoms of water [depending on the state of the tide]. The channel to the westward of the rock is both narrower and shoaler, having only 3 or 4 fathoms in it at low water ...

I go into this detail for good reason, for I want to be as certain in my mind as possible that I am following the track sailing vessels seeking urgent shelter would take; so the westward channel is the one *Spray* takes, above the very same ground over which great historic figures have sailed.

Great historic figures, do I say? I go further and imagine *Spray* and I are coming in with one of the very greatest. Read this now, and sink back into the sixteenth century and take station behind him, take station behind Sir Francis Drake soon after the start of his incredible round-the-world voyage in 1577: and delight in the fact that this is an eye-witness account of an occasion almost unknown to the Cornish of today.

I quote from Hakluyt's *Summarie and True Discourse of the Famous Voyage of Sir Francis Drake, into the South Sea, and therehence about the whole Globe of the earth, begun in the Yeere of our Lord, 1577.*

> The 15 day of November [1577], M. Francis Drake, with a fleete of five ships and barkes, and to the number of 164 men, gentlemen and sailers, departed from Plimmouth, giving out his pretended voyage for Alexandria: but the wind falling contrary hee was forced the next morning to put into Falmouth [then only a hamlet] haven in Cornewall, where such and so terrible a tempest tooke us, as few men have seen the like and was indeed so vehement that all our ships were likely to have gone to wracke: but it pleased God to preserve us from that extremitie, and to afflict us only for that present with these two particulars: The mast of our Admirall which

was the *Pelican* was cut overboored for the safeguard of the
ship, and the *Mariegold* was driven ashore, and somewhat
bruised: for the repairing of which damages wee returned
again to Plimmouth, and having recovered these harmes,
and brought the ships againe to good state, we set forth the
second time from Plimmouth, and set sail the 13 day of
December following ....

My historical view of Falmouth is enriched when I gaze across
the water from the vantage point on Pendennis above the
dockyard, and wonder at what point the storm drove the vessels
toward the banks and destruction, only to be saved
miraculously at the last moment. Even so, the *Mariegold* was
actually driven ashore, and surely the *Pelican* would have suffered the same fate had Drake not cut down his mast to decrease
the windage on the harassed vessel, dragging its anchor until
this drastic (though normal) remedy was effected, lessening the
pull on the anchor.

How exciting it is to be in *Spray* now, visualising accompany-
ing on this water the five vessels (none over 100 tons), when
Drake had to endure what must have been monumental
frustration and dismay at the very beginning of such a
momentous, hazardous voyage.

Incidentally, a word is not out of place here on this remarkable man, Richard Hakluyt, whose work has been an absolute
treasure house for historians studying the great period of the
sixteenth and seventeenth centuries when England was playing
a major role in the conquest of the oceans and in world
discovery.

Hakluyt can be lightly compared to a man of today with a
tape-recorder who captures, from eye-witnesses of major and
minor events, interviews with men who were on the spot, pre-
serving the substance of the event for all time.

He was born in Herefordshire, about 1550, and educated at
Westminster School and Christ Church, Oxford. Here he took
Holy Orders in a half-hearted way, for he soon felt he wanted to
spread the wings of his learning to be able to collect and study

the accounts of those voyages that were then being made by France, Portugal and Spain, in particular. He studied Greek, Latin, Italian, Spanish, Portuguese, and French, and by the time he was thirty was equipped to do something about the waywardness of the English in terms of voyages of discovery compared to those of the foregoing.

In 1582, he published *Divers Voyages touching the Discovery of America*, a book which attracted much attention among the English establishment. This was a precursor of his great work which occupied him for many years, succeeding editions of *The Principal Navigations, Voyages, Traffiques and Discoveries of the English Nation*. For these he interviewed the survivors of many expeditions, taking down, word for word, statements from all levels of status, from captain to cabin boy.

Towards the end of his life he reverted to his original calling, and took a living in Suffolk, subsequently becoming Archdeacon of Westminster. He died in 1616, having lived long enough to see the rise of England to sovereign of the seas. He was buried in Westminster Abbey.

I have already quoted from Hakluyt's opening account of Drake's circumnavigation of the world, which he completed in just under three years. Drake did not return to Falmouth, but the part in his rescue from disaster that the open arms of this fair haven of Cornwall played in its success always invests in me a tingling of pride as *Spray* passes through the channel between Black Rock and St Anthony's Point. On this occasion, I intend to anchor off Trefusis Point, under the lee of Pendennis, where the channel leads to Penryn.

Falmouth, at the time of Drake's visit, consisted of only a few cottages; and Sir John Killigrew was only then contemplating the building of Arwenack House (now happily renovated) and the creation of Falmouth to take the trade from Penryn. In due course, the family was successful in this, but it was not until 1650 that the Customs House was finally established in Falmouth, thus drawing much valued trade from what had been the flourishing port of Penryn. I shall be returning to the Killigrews in a moment.

Spray is now approaching the spot where we are going to anchor, and where in 1814, during the Peninsular War, a troop-ship, the *Queen*, bringing soldiers of Wellington's army home from Lisbon, dropped anchor.

Onboard was a cross-section of those left behind by the tide of war. The list of passengers, many of whom were families, was:

180 invalid soldiers
63 women
58 children
10 French prisoners.

Crew members, and others, made up a total of 332 persons each one of whom had endured anxiety for the future, fears for the present. Each one must have thanked God for being in home waters at last with only a run up the Channel after a brief call here in Falmouth for watering and re-victualling.

The *Queen* had arrived in Falmouth on 11th January 1814. She soon received orders to sail for Portsmouth on 15th January, but she was destined never to leave. I leave it to the reporter on the *West Briton* to give his dramatic report:

Headed 'A Melancholy Catastrophe', he went on to observe that 'The storm that raged when our paper went to press this day's night did not spread its fury in vain ...

The ship *Queen*, Captain Carr, belonging to London, a transport bound from Lisbon and Cadiz to Portsmouth, with invalids from Lord Wellington's army, put into Falmouth on se'nnight, and remained at a single anchor from that time to the Thursday following.

On that day a gale commenced which continued with increasing violence until between four and five o'clock on Friday morning, when, after drifting her anchor for some time, she parted her cable and drifted on shore at Trefusis Point, where she became a complete wreck in 20 minutes after she struck.

At this awful moment, there were upwards of 380 persons on board who, having escaped the dangers of the Peninsular

War, were returning to their native land after years of active service in a foreign clime. Many of the Officers and Soldiers were accompanied by their wives and children, of whom the number was more than 120.

Some of the passengers, alarmed by the confusion that reigned on deck, had come up undressed immediately after the vessel had parted her anchor, but it was only to ascertain that it was impossible to save the ship. An attempt was made to let go the other anchor, but before it could be accomplished the vessel struck.

The horror and confusion that ensued was indescribable – those who got on deck were either swept off by the waves which swept over the wreck with great violence, or maimed by the fragments of the rigging and spars that flew about in all directions. A number could not make their way up, and as the vessel's bottom was speedily beaten to pieces, they were drowned or crushed to death by the floating planks and timbers.

In a short time the ship went to pieces which, being driven against the shore in all directions, dealt destruction to many of those who were still contending with the fury of the elements.

Some of the unfortunate sufferers who had got on shore as soon as the vessel struck ran to the little town of Flushing, the inhabitants of which were immediately alarmed, and whilst some stayed to receive and accommodate the naked fugitives, others hastened to the wreck, as did all the farmers etc. in the neighbourhood, who were eager to afford assistance to those who were washed ashore.

The return of day presented a shocking spectacle to the crowd that now surrounded the fatal spot: dead bodies of many women and children, many of them mangled, several hundred of them naked, and some of them scarcely half dressed, strewed the shore – it has been ascertained that *two hundred and thirteen* perished.

Such of the bodies that were found have been interred in a becoming manner.

May I counsel the reader that the true plight of these poor victims of the storm can only be imagined if you remember it was happening in the dark, in winter. Further – and this is only for the seaman fully to understand from experience – the fearful reality of a storm at sea is not just the cold, the wetness, the weight of the wind, the driving spray, but the *noise*, a relentless screaming from the rigging, the furious weighted swish, rising and falling, of the frustrated waves, slapping and swamping anything in their way – and the *noise*, always the noise.

To this was added for these poor folk the brutality of being picked up and thrown about, onto the pebbled foreshore, into one another, unrecognisable, wreckage maiming the already maimed, lungs choked with water – and always the *noise*!

And now the reporter again:

A lieut. Daniels, of the 30th regiment, got on shore, though much bruised, but his wife and five children perished.

Of ten French prisoners-of-war who were on board four have been saved. Amongst the melancholy appearances which so many dead bodies presented, the hearts of those who witnessed the shocking scene, were particularly affected by the sight of the corpse of a lovely female, wife to one of the officers washed on shore, with that of her infant which, even in death, she held clasped to her bosom.

The exertions of the persons whom the cries of their drowning fellow creatures brought to the Point deserve every praise: but those of two individuals merit particular notice. Geo. G. Fox Esq. of Falmouth, no sooner heard of the wreck than he despatched his servants to prepare his house at Trefusis, for the reception of such of the sufferers that might be saved, and hastened himself to the spot, where he remained affording every assistance in order to save as many lives and preserve as much of the property belonging to the vessel and passengers as possible. Mr Plomer, a respectable farmer who resides at Trefusis, also hastened to the spot, and having collected his labourers rendered essential assistance to those who reached the shore alive, many of whom were so much bruised as to be unable to move, and but for timely assistance would have perished.

Tonight, when I lie in my bunk thinking on this wreck, in *Spray* lying to her anchor in the same area as the *Queen* must have been, a thought keeps intruding into my mind. Isn't it conceivable that this might be the place where Drake brought his ships in to shelter?

Unlikely? Perhaps. But if wind, tide and visibility had been the same on that day in 1577 as when the *Queen* came in, in 1814, his choice might have been shaped by these similar influences to anchor just here.

In these waters there must have been many dramas played out, but none so symptomatic of the times as that undertaken by Lady Jane Killigrew, the rather murky wife of Sir John who was busy making local enemies as a result of his success in gaining support in high places, including that of good King James himself, for his creation of Falmouth.

In 1737, Martin Killigrew wrote a history of this active and influential family of the Falmouth/Helford/Lizard environment. Today, there is no Killigrew in Cornwall. It has simply died away.

In passing, I might mention the strange way that there are a number of great Cornish families that have had roots take hold over the centuries in the Cornish soil, have grown like flowers to full bloom, and then have died away and disappeared: such names as Arundell, Trevanion, Basset and Grenville, Godolphin and Killigrew. [For Borlase on this, see Appendix A.]

Yes, Martin Killigrew wrote the family history in 1737, in which he introduces us to the Lady Jane. Referring to the trying time Sir John had had in getting his licence to develop what is now Falmouth, Martin says that Sir John had hardly got over this before he 'fell under much greater affliction, the prostitution of his wife'.

This lady, the daughter of Sir George Forman, of

Northampton, of a family 'new in the peerage', contrived to have an affair with the Governor of Pendennis Castle, or, in Martin's vividly picturesque phrase, he 'debauched' her.

> Arrived to that shameful degree, [he wrote] the cuckolded husband, in point of honour and for quietness of mind, found himself under a necessity to prosecute a divorce from her in the Archbishop's Court, which lasted so many years and was so very expensive, as quite ruined the estate, to the degree of being often put to very hard shifts to get home from London upon the frequent recesses in the process.
>
> This woman in such long contest was in no degree protected by her family, but supported and cherished by the town of Penryn, from their jealousy and hatred of Arwenack [Killigrew], as specially appears to this day by plate by her given to the Mayor and Corporation of Penryn.

It was another Lady Killigrew (Mary), grandmother of Sir John, who had earlier shown a talent for notoriety in the district, a colourful one which brought her in fearsome contact with the law.

The facts of this case were related by the Cornish historian, William Hals (1655-1737) and published in 1750. I do not intend to dwell on this account, for, though it had a basis of accuracy, it was subsequently discovered to be mostly false.

The truth was ferreted out by H. Michell Whitley from documents at the Public Record Office; and I in turn have ferreted his account out of the *Journal of the Royal Institution of Cornwall*, vol VII, July, 1883.

He first counsels the reader to 'remember that England in Queen Elizabeth's time was far different to the "present day". If there was one feeling more deeply inwrought than any other into the nerve and fibre of the average Englishman, it was hatred of the Pope, the Inquisition, and the Spaniard.'

The western seas swarmed with pirates who without the open sanction of the Queen attacked the vessels and weakened the power of Spain.

On 1st January 1582, the *Mary*, of San Sebastian, a Spanish ship of 144 tons burden, owned by John de Chavis and Philip de Oryo, merchants, the latter being the captain, arrived in Falmouth haven, and anchored under Arwenack House.

Here, for 'lack of Wynde it remained', the owners staying at an inn in Penryn, awaiting a change.

About midnight on 7th January, the ship was boarded by a boatful of men who overpowered the Spanish sailors, and set sail; the Spaniards appear to have been thrown overboard and the ship taken to Ballentynmoor, in Ireland, where she was plundered. Formal complaint of their loss by the owners, the Commissioners of Piracy in Cornwall (who comprised among others, Sir John Killigrew, Sir Francis Godolphin and Mr Chamond) held a meeting at Penryn to enquire into the complaint.

Suspicion appears to have fallen on some of Sir John Killigrew's servants who bore rather a bad name for dealing with pirates, and two of them, Hawkins and Kendall, were thought to be the culprits; but one Elizabeth Bowden, who kept a small inn at Penryn, having deposed that these men were at her house there until twelve o'clock on the night of the attack, the jury returned the open verdict that the ship had been stolen, but by whom there was no evidence to show.

No doubt it would have been convenient for the matter to have been dropped there, but Chavis and de Oryo were men of action, and having procured a safe conduct to London from the Commissioners, they laid their complaint before higher authorities, with the result that the Earl of Bedford instructed Sir Richard Grenville and Mr Edmund Tremayne to make a searching investigation into the matter.

Briefly, the story as narrated by witness after witness was that the plot originated with Dame Killigrew who, on the Sunday in question, ordered Hawkins and Kendall to go and board the Spanish vessel. The Governor of the rival castle to Pendennis, namely, St Mawes, testified that one of Sir John Killigrew's men came with the news that the Spanish ship was about to weigh anchor, and also requested him not to prevent her doing so.

The two men joined up with other sailors who had been waiting all day at Pendennis Castle, of which Sir John Killigrew was then Governor.

After an unsuccessful attempt to get the two Spaniards to rejoin their ship (so that no witness would be left behind to tell the tale) the party went onboard, successfully overcoming and tying up those of the crew who were there.

About midnight they set sail and, on leaving the harbour, lowered a boat, putting Kendall and Hawkins together with plunder to be taken back by them for giving to Lady Killigrew and Mrs Killigrew: also to the maids and servants in the house and to two ladies in Penryn. Lady Killigrew was very discontented at the meagre supply of goods her husband had sent her so she kept much of the share allotted to the others.

We are not told in detail what form the plunder took except that there were 'sundry bolts of Hollands and packs of leather'. We do know, however, that the leather which was part of Lady Killigrew's spoil, she put in a cask to keep, buried in the garden at Arwenack. Those in the know were warned by my lady to tell no one of their treasure, for if the facts became known they were liable to be hanged.

Some hundred years later, in 1670, Sir Peter Killigrew built a new quay at Falmouth (still virtually no more than a hamlet) thus exploiting the marvellous harbour formed by the mouth of the River Fal for ships of all kinds; of commerce, of war, and, yes, of the Falmouth packets, the long distance mail carriers of the GPO, to Lisbon, the Brazils, the West Indies and America.

I draw now from Lysons, in his *Magna Britannia,* vol iii, when the packets had been operating some 120 years. This is how the service grew, through dangerous times at sea when England was at almost continual war. Lysons lists (1810) the origins of this Post Office organisation (not naval) thus:

Falmouth owes much of its prosperity to the establishment of the post office packets to Lisbon, the West Indies etc. In 1705 five packets were employed between Falmouth and the West Indies, [96 days round trip] the vessels were of 150 tons and manned with thirty men. Two years afterwards the same number of packets were employed between Falmouth and Lisbon [15 days]; in 1755, five packets were employed between Falmouth and New York [90 days].

During the next few years the service increased to include Corunna, Gibraltar and Malta; and Black Rock featured in the passage of everyone of them as the emblem of arrival or departure, with the tangled emotions of farewell or hurrah from those on board.

All through the eighteenth century the links that bound Falmouth to the Post Office service grew steadily stronger. As the numbers of ships increased so the local tradesmen prospered. The demand for stores was incessant, most of which (due to poor communication) had to be provided locally. The use of the packets as carriers of mail, and gold and silver bullion, was invaluable for merchants and Government alike. In addition nearly 3,000 passengers were carried yearly. But it was hazardous for the vessels and crews (and passengers) who suffered those attacks from privateers and ships of war.

We have not room here to delve into the fascinating story of this glamorous, courageous (and sometimes corrupt, be it said), civilian service on whom demands were made on those taking part not dissimilar to the tension experienced by Commandos today; for example, repelling boarders in hand-to-hand fighting on the heaving decks of two ships grappled together.

However, there will be room here for me to take you on board a packet to be shown, by a member of the crew, a glimpse of his life style.

Samuel Kelly was a St Ives man born in June 1764, and he joined his first packet in 1781, probably a vessel of 150 tons and carrying 12 six-pounder guns. We have been introduced to Sam by Crosbie Garstin in his book comprising his *Journal* (Jonathan Cape, 1925):

In this ship I was stationed when at sea in the main-top

[some 60 feet high] even when the ship has been rolling nearly gunwale in, and often pitching with very sudden jerks against a head sea, but through mercy I was never thrown out of the top ...

When I was in the packets at Falmouth there were twenty-four armed packets (based) on Falmouth most of which had from fourteen to eighteen guns (and two with twenty-six guns).

One night, when in my hammock on board, asleep, I felt a cold hand on my thigh, which did not alarm me a little as there was only one man on board that slept regularly in the betwixt decks. The ship was much infested with rats which made great noises at night ...

I have counted thirteen packets in Falmouth at one time. These vessels seldom rejected any able-bodied landsmen that offered themselves as they were cheaper than seamen, requiring only 16s. to 18s. per month. These ships were therefore receptacles for a number of dissolute and depraved young men who were either ashamed or afraid to continue in their native place in the County of Cornwall. These newcomers, having no home in Falmouth, were generally victualled on board in harbour and slept round the galley fire at night without bedding ...

As we drew near Newfoundland we experienced much fog and rain and as I had little clothing and a long time in a warm climate I suffered severely not being able to dry my jacket, or even my shirt, the weather being so wet. The foresail being directly over the scuttle descending our habitation conducted the wind down in such a torrent on our wet bodies that it made us tremble with cold and two or three of our crew were laid to the deep which was much felt as our ship required much pumping.

I have gone below wet and for want of a change of clothes have been afraid to go to bed, dreading what I should experience in turning out of my bed in a bath of sweat occasioned by going to sleep in a wet shirt and then putting on again my wet jacket and trousers to keep my watch on deck. I have in preference to turning into my hammock during my four hours below, sat down on a chest with my arms across shivering and shaking with the wind pouring down on my wet clothes ...

During the American War three fire ships were laying in Falmouth Roads and at about two o'clock on a fine day I saw smoke arising from one of the ships' main hatchways, which continued increasing till I saw fire running up the shrouds and she was soon ablaze.

When the guns got hot their shots were discharged at the town and country. The other ships slipped and went to sea, about four o'clock she exploded with a tremendous noise and great concussion. When her cables burnt she drove on shore opposite the town, and as my chamber window commanded her about ten at night I saw her whole length glowing to the water's edge.

Now here is another point of view. James Silk Buckingham wrote in his autobiography that:

No spot in England in which so limited a surface among so small a number in the aggregate, were to be seen so much of the gaiety and elegance of life as in this little village of Flushing. Officers with long square-tail coats with large buttons on pockets and sleeves; square-toed shoes with massive silver buckles, and cocked hats. The boats' crews with blue jackets and trousers, and bright scarlet waistcoats, overlaid with gilt buttons. The streets sparkled with gold epaulets, gold laced hats and brilliant uniforms. Often the packets would be berthed, one at each side of the quay, either to be scrubbed or paid off. This was the time the whole village went gay, forgetting the past, and with no regard to what might happen on their next voyage.

These were brave people, for it must be remembered that many packets left the port never to return, including the *Hearty*, *Ariel*, *Recruit*, *Redpole*, *Thais*, *Calypso*, *Bresies*, *Melville* and *Lady Hobart*. It is recorded that between eighty and ninety widows were counted at one period of Flushing's history as belonging to members of packet crews. A safe return, therefore, was welcomed with dinners, balls, etc., held at captains' houses (or on the deck of a packet), and every night dances were in full force in the long rooms attached to public houses.

Owing to the plentiful supplies of wines and spirits which were smuggled ashore at the end of each voyage, no one considered drinking unbecoming, but rather the mark of a gentleman. It was thought a mean sort of hospitality to allow a guest at a great house to leave in any sort of a sober state.

*

Spray and I are now bidding this fair haven of Falmouth, this world-famous harbour, neatly provided by Cornwall for ocean navigators for a thousand years, yes, we are bidding it sadly farewell.

Black Rock is a half mile astern on our starboard quarter. There is quite a breeze and grey cloud, grey sea, and *Spray* is lifting to the swell, rising and falling among the grey hills and hollows, sails taut in a dancing pattern of sweeping parabolas swinging against the sky.

As always, I feel conscious of the link this water gives me with the countless seamen who cleaved through the water where *Spray* is now; some thankful, after a long hazardous voyage, to see Black Rock, others with heavy heart, watching it slowly fade out of sight, while yet others with no thought but their duty.

One such I see, in my mind now. She is the *Pickle*, flying the flag of the Royal Navy, a frigate leaning to the wind, schooner rigged, her sails full, and she is sailing as fast as she can, no question of shortening sail, even with Falmouth so near. My word, she's in a hurry. Let's see what she's about.

*

It is a grey November morning in the year 1805, and the *Pickle* was carrying urgent despatches for the Admiralty from Admiral Collingwood.

She was bringing the first news of the Battle of Trafalgar which had been won twelve days before. She was bringing news, also, of the tragic death of the Commander-in-Chief, Admiral Lord Nelson.

Communications being what they were, it would still be at least two days before London would hear the news. Today, both news of the event and its reception in England would occur on the same day. In 1805, the action was on 23rd October, and the first newspaper report of it on 11th November.

Readers of the West Country newspaper, *Sherborne Mercury* got two columns on that day devoted to reporting what had appeared in the *London Gazette Extraordinary* of 6th November.

The Royal Cornwall Gazette, on the other hand, with naval connections on the spot in Falmouth, its birthplace, was able to give an immediacy to the news which was akin to that of the Special Correspondent of today.

To supplement, if not to supplant, the hand-out from the Admiralty through the *London Gazette Extraordinary*, the Cornish paper was able to give news with a Truro dateline.

The *Sherborne Mercury* even two days later and nineteen days after the battle, was limited to the official news; but the Cornish paper could present it editorially thus:

Truro – Saturday, November 9. We have this week to announce a battle more tremendous, and a conquest more glorious, than even the proud annals of the British Navy could boast till now. But Lord Nelson is no more: his ardent soul departed to heaven on the wings of Victory.

The important intelligence was brought into Falmouth by the *Pickle* schooner, Lieutenant Lapenotière who proceeded immediately through Truro to London. We were therefore in hopes that last night's post could have brought us the official details of this splendid action; but there was not time for the printing of the *London Gazette* before the post left the Capital.

The writer of the paper's story was referring to the Admiralty summary (which did, in fact, arrive just before going to press) and informs his readers that it confirms all the leading features of the glorious conquest, and to these 'we shall add such other particulars as we have received through private channels'.

The subscribers, beset for years by bloody wars on the Continent, with the spectre of invincible Napoleon as yet undiminished, the French and Lowland ports filled with transports, and invasion of England expected any minute, read this eclectic news of an overwhelming victory in the following manner:

Lord Nelson's signal for battle was accompanied by another which implied that 'England expected every man to do his duty'. When this was explained to several ships' crews, they answered it with three cheers.

The combined fleets of France and Spain had added to their crews several thousand soldiers. *The Santissima Trinidada* (the largest ship in the world then) carrying 146 guns and 2,500 men, was fought at close quarters and sunk by the tremendous fire-power of the *Victory*.

Lord Nelson was pointing out to his officers the gallant conduct of Admiral Collingwood at the 'moment he received the fatal ball. He had just said, "If we all do our duty, like him, it will be a glorious day for old England".'

There follows another story from the Plymouth correspondent whither the *Pickle* had sailed after dropping off Lapenotière at Falmouth with his despatches.

The correspondent with information 'straight from the Admiral's Office' mainly confines himself to elaborating on the casualties. He concludes, Plymouth faces seem to be in mourning for the loss of our gallant, ever to be lamented Admiral; 'tis a dear bought victory'.

This astute correspondent somehow contrived to trace the recipient of a private letter from an officer in the *Euryalus* to someone in Plymouth, and brought by the *Pickle*. The sense of no ordinary scoop is as alive today as it was then, dated 22nd October. It reads:

Sir, I scarcely know whether, after so great a loss as the
nation has sustained in Lord Nelson, and every one of us a
friend, added to the inevitable destruction of 19 fine prizes
[wrecked in a gale on a lee shore after the battle], I ought to
congratulate you – but since the enemy, minus so many
ships, and we, I trust, not one, even in that there is matter to
rejoice. Such a victory, under such circumstances so
disadvantageous to the attack, never was achieved. Admiral
Villeneuve (the French C-in-C) who is now at my elbow can
scarcely yet credit it, and his despair and grief exceeds anything I ever saw.

I did not leave the *Victory* till the shot were flying thick over
her, and the last signal Lord Nelson made was such as
cannot and never will be forgot – I have time for no more, the
vessel is going, but I shall soon see you, as I am to carry home
the [captured] Admirals.

In another letter one has a picture of those unhappy admirals,
their lofty pride and the destruction of a supremely confidently
mounted attack on England of immense proportions all laid
low in one unbelievable afternoon.

The letter I quote is from the *London Gazette Extraordinary* of
6th November from Collingwood to the Admiralty.

I have taken Admiral Villeneuve into the ship. Vice Admiral
Don Aliva is dead. Whenever the temper of the weather will
permit, and I can spare a frigate [for there were only four in
action with the fleet], I shall collect the other Flag Officers
and send them off to England with their flags (if they do not
all go to the bottom) to be laid at His Majesty's feet. I am
etc., Collingwood.

There are one or two endpieces to this story which are of
interest.

First, the final wording of Nelson's famous signal was chosen
by the Admiral with the humble help of the Signal Midshipman
of the *Victory* who (for several code reasons) suggested England

expects rather than *confides*. His name was John Pollard, a Cornishman from Kingsand.

This son of Cornwall also had the distinction of shooting, from the poop of the *Victory*, the Frenchman who had killed Nelson. The second-in-command of the *Pickle*, Lieutenant John Kingdon, was also a Cornishman; and Laponetière subsequently married a girl from Liskeard. We may be sure that she was called upon, on occasions, to console her gallant husband's abiding sense of chagrin embedded in the fact that, at the same time as he arrived at the Admiralty with his despatches, there also arrived a messenger who had raced by land from Oporto. The Consul had sent him.

Disappointing as that experience must have been, being all but pipped at the post, Laponetière must have had some slight consolation: for though the despatches themselves arrived at the same time as those carried by the Consul's messenger, the actual news of the battle would have reached the Admiralty shortly after the *Pickle* arrived in Plymouth from dropping off Laponetière in Falmouth.

I should quickly qualify this for the reason that the Admiralty Telegraph system of a chain of signal stations to the naval ports might not have been in operation in time for use in 1805. I have yielded to the temptation of assuming the system to Plymouth *was* in being then, on the basis of an old print referred to in the Journal of the Society of Nautical Research (*Mariner's Mirror*), vol. xxiv, 1938.

The print is of the Admiralty building drawn from the Horse Guards parade ground and dated 1st March 1805. It shows the existence of two shutter machines.

Confirming this evidence of the existence of this signals system at the time is a letter, dated Christmas Day 1805, referring to the extension of the Telegraph from London to Plymouth to be extended to Falmouth. This letter is from Admiral Barham to Admiral Cornwallis in which he says, 'We have ordered a Telegraph from Plymouth to Falmouth which must prove very convenient.'

The foregoing appears among the *Barham Papers*, Pt. III, and is in Commander Hilary Mead's paper on the 'Admiralty Telegraphs and Semaphores', the original being in the keeping of the Society of Nautical Research.

The Telegraph of 1805 was an elaborate arrangement erected above the roof of the Telegraph building and rising to some 50 feet. It consisted of an arrangement of slabs of wood encased in a framework on the principle of a Venetian blind, so that each slab could be moved at will.

By 1820, these cumbersome 'instruments' were being replaced at all naval coastal signal stations by the 3-armed semaphore.

These stations were placed on higher levels of ground every four to five miles and a coded signal could be sent from Plymouth to the Admiralty, and a reply received, in little more than twenty minutes, visibility being good. A message to Portsmouth was received back in half that time.

In this day and age, the twentieth century, Cornwall has played a vast part on behalf of the nation in providing the means of communication to and from far distant places all over the world. Its geological and geographical position is uniquely favourable for electronic signals; and so it was that in the beginning of this century Marconi chose Poldhu, in the Lizard Peninsula, for his long distance experiments with his invention, the 'wireless', and it was from there he achieved his goal of sending the first messages to America. From Poldhu the huge post office satellite bowl on Goonhilly Downs is now plainly visible, but instead of being content with a message to America it sweeps the sky like a fisherman with a net, hauling in catches from all over the world and outer space. And for this Cornwall outbid all other locations in the country.

Yes, it has for long been thus. Cornwall has been first in the field in the world communications business, were it ship, radio, telegraph or telephone the medium. Only the civil, as opposed to the naval and military aeroplane, finds no spectacular home in Cornwall.

Not so very long ago, *Spray* (now rather restlessly waiting to know when we are going to get on course toward Plymouth), passed a shy, demure little village, near Land's End, which is now well known for its open air theatre on the cliff-top, nearby.

That little village, Porthcurno, is a place of unique distinction, for here was the exit point of the first of the cables that were to span routes of communication all over the British Empire, thousands and thousands of miles of it, all painstakingly laid over the ocean bed in miraculous manner, and then feeding the country with immediate contact with the other side of the world. Even with the coming of radio, the cable network was too precious to be allowed to suffer.

And why am I thinking of this little village while *Spray* is still sailing on a course out to sea when surely it is time for us to continue our cruise along the south coast eastward? Well, two things are nagging me, and I feel we must retrace our path from Land's End. Let me explain why.

III

Porthcurno and the Winged Word

I suppose it is reasonable when you feel you have completed a project, to wish you had covered it differently, or that you had included something you've left out.

Well, I feel I have omitted introducing you to the men who worked at Porthcurno on the very beginnings of the Cable Telegraph Company, a Cornish concern centred on this village whose work has had an immense influence on the development of world communications in the century and a quarter it has been training men for duty in far distant places.

Also nagging me is that we failed to meet Humphry Davy (1778–1829) of Penzance, when *Spray* was in Mount's Bay during our call there as recorded in my previous book, *Cornwall and the Tumbling Sea*.

My reason for this omission, wholly inadequate, was that I have always had a blockage in my mind over Sir Humphry, partly because the name 'Humphry' must take me back to some tedious episode in my childhood, and partly for the shaming fact that I had heard so many times he was the inventor of the miner's safety lamp I closed my eyes and ears to the fact that he was one of the most influential Cornishmen the Duchy has produced: added to which, the breadth of his interests and achievements, and his personality, make him fascinating to meet.

My mind is made up. I say aloud to *Spray*, come on, round we go, and I pull the tiller up so she swings to starboard. I haul in on the sheets to keep the wind in the sails, and then pull them taut as we wear ship, and the boom swings to the lee side. I haul in on the staysail and jib sheets and now, here we are, heeling to port with an air of purpose as opposed to the relative stillness when wind comes from astern as we have been having till now. Her bow points westward to the Lizard.

My purpose is to cross the wide mouth of Mount's Bay, and then sail along the length of the cultivated sloping cliffs, with their neat, protective paddocks of the market gardens and their honeycombed hedges. Then, just as the coast turns up toward Land's End by the Runnelstone Rock, we will sail on to Porthcurno.

There are white horses on the rumpled sea now, and *Spray* is cutting through them, gaily, superbly confident. The wind is getting up a bit, and often there is a flurry of spray that falls with a playful plop on the deck.

The grey cloud is dispersing and the sun is smiling on us as we speed through the water a half mile off the rugged, dangerous coast. I look forward to seeing Porthcurno. We shall be there in about an hour, about four o'clock.

The first of the cables laid from Cornwall ran from Sennen Cove (just the other side on the north coast) to St Mary's, Scilly Islands. This was in 1869. At the same time surveys were made, by the Eastern Telegraph Co, all along the south coast to find a more suitable spot, one which would serve not only as the point where cables would enter the water, but also as a base and training centre. This was found at Porthcurno.

In 1870 a cable was laid along the seabed to Malta, some 1,000 miles away, and this was the first stage of a project of monumental proportions, namely, a cable to Australia. Within a year it had been extended to Singapore, and in November 1872, the line was open to Australia.

Two ships were engaged at a time when laying cable, each carrying 1,800 miles of it onboard at a time (yes, eighteen hundred miles).

Meanwhile, at Porthcurno, sixty young educated bachelors were confined in this out of the way spot. They were understandably restless, to say the least, and soon we have the managing director having difficulty in keeping the young bloods in order.

Football was played in an endeavour to make things more tolerable; and it is a fact that when the trainees and staff were sent off to their first station abroad, it was likely to be to Vigo they would go, for here there was the first overseas station of the company. It is an almost certainty that it was these young men who first introduced the game of football into Portugal; if so, that is another 'first' for Cornwall.

I draw my information mainly from Hugh Barty King's book, *Girdle Round the Earth*, (Heinemann). At one Christmas, the managing director felt it necessary to read out the following to the assembled staff and we are told it was not an isolated event:

I have heard with great regret upon three occasions within the last two months, that some of our staff are conspicuous for the use of bad language and drinking. Now, I am by no means willing to learn that I cannot control a number of young Gentlemen at a station in England, any or all of whom I have the power of replacing at a very short notice.

In a memo of this time the director wrote of his concern that:

Up to this day in this year nineteen cases have been brought before me of messages having the wrong station 'to' upon them. This is so serious an error and so needless, that I insist upon such negligence being at once stopped. I will do my best to trace out these nineteen errors and bring them home to the men who committed them. This inexcusable carelessness loses us many customers and brings disgrace ... There are such gross mistakes as Alexandria for Malta, London for Manchester, Calcutta for Colombo ...

And here is another reproof:

The Managing Director is much disappointed to learn that many of the staff habitually neglect to attend Divine Service on Sundays. This should not be; a man who neglects his first religious duties will end by neglecting his duties to his neighbours and employers. The MD therefore expects every man will go to some place of Divine Worship every Sunday when off duty. A return must be made to HQ every week of those who attend Church for the information of the MD.

In March 1877, Mrs Emma Bull, the wife of an executive, wrote to one of her children at a time when her husband was unsuccessfully trying to maintain order at the station.

There is a telegraph station near Land's End, put down in a secluded bay, and no doubt lonely in these days when men of every station in society require so much amusement and excitement. The Company have furnished it with a billiard table, library, etc. and now it is a kind of school preparing young men for positions abroad.

But just now the whole community are at loggerheads, each with all the others. Sir James Anderson [Captain of the *Great Eastern* when laying 2,500 miles of cable across the Atlantic] went down but did no good amongst them so he came back and said nothing.

Matters went worse and he sent a clerk to try and soothe them but no good effect followed, and at last he had to confess the whole story. So your father has gone down, and the probability he may disperse the whole colony. I expect his having to stay till Tuesday. The weather is bad and this is perhaps as good a way of spending his Easter as any he could find.

Fortunately, it was not deemed necessary to 'disperse the whole colony'.

The contrast between the laxity of discipline and the importance of the task the young men were engaged on was certainly pronounced, but in some directions they were to improve: for example, it was not necessary to repeat reference to the following rather sordid picture. On the notice board one morning was a notice to this effect: 'Complaints are made to me

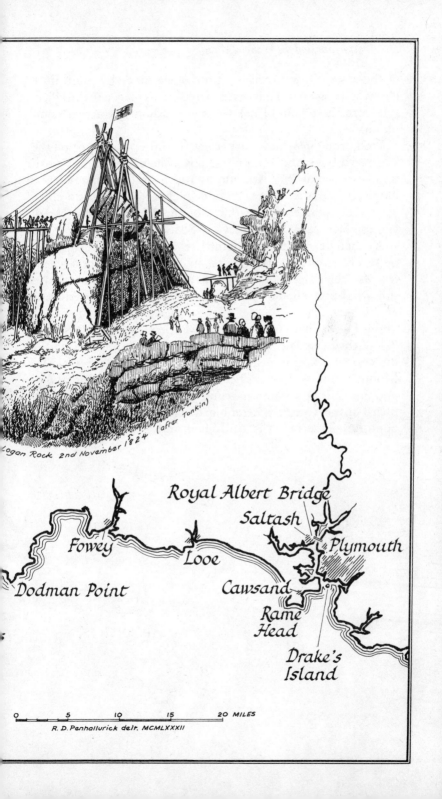

Logan Rock 2nd November 1824 (after Tonkin)

Royal Albert Bridge

Saltash

Plymouth

Fowey

Looe

Dodman Point

Cawsand

Rame
Head

Drake's
Island

0   5   10   15   20 MILES

R. D. Penhallurick delt. MCMLXXXII

of the state of the firegrate in the office made by night duty clerks spitting on it. I have had two spitoons placed in the office, therefore there should not be any occasion for further complaints.'

Well, from *Spray* now we can see the little village just off the starboard bow, and I am conscious of its extraordinary position, exposed to the Atlantic as much as the Channel, the names in the area that surround it, those of rocks and cliffs, clearly defining the ruggedness of the scene: Cribba Head, Gamper, Horrace, Vessacks, Carn Scathe, Hella Point.

As though to press the point I realise the wind has got up quite a bit, and *Spray* is enjoying an increasing liveliness, eager to shake herself clear of restrictions of rocks and coastline and to sail, wind-pressed, out the way she is heading, into the Atlantic and freedom.

But I have different ideas. I am wanting to get into Penzance before they close the inner harbour, and with the wind in the direction it is now it means *Spray* will need at least two tacks up Mount's Bay. So I swing her round to starboard to go about, and her sails shiver and flap and ripple as she goes from starboard to port tack, quietening down as I settle her on the opposite course, her sails wind-filled, and she, happy again.

IV

Humphry Davy, Singular Scientist

Mount's Bay now lies open to port. With this rising wind from the north-west we won't be able to fetch Penzance on one tack as I thought, but *Spray* is holding nicely to the wind and we'll be able to stay on course until off St Michael's Mount. Then, one small tack, and in twenty minutes we should be off the Penzance basin. I look at my watch. Yes, with any luck we should be there before the pontoon closes. If necessary we'll get into Newlyn and spend the night there. The sea is quite bouncy now and visibility is falling and there's a heavy rain-cloud over Penwith.

Among the other books I carry with me on board *Spray* are the usual navigational ones, but there is also an unusual one. Fellow seamen may find it rather eccentric, but nevertheless they will concede its interest. Let me explain.

When I am travelling I add an extra dimension to the interest offered me by the journey, by carrying an early guide book as well as a contemporary one, and it is the former that has the place of priority.

For example, when on holiday on the island of Skye, a land relatively untouched by modern influences, I took as my guide book not the one on sale at the hotel I passed the night in on the mainland, but Boswell's *Tour of the Hebrides*; and when we took passage in the coastal steamer that plies from Bergen, on the Norwegian coast, calling at all the townships along it up to the North Cape and round to the Russian frontier, I took with me Winston Churchill's account of the Norwegian Campaign of 1940.

Likewise in *Spray* I take as my *Channel Pilot* a copy of the edition written before the general use of steam and which pertained to the navigation of sailing vessels. My copy was first published over a century ago, in 1859.

And what does it say of Mount's Bay, and how, in this deteriorating visibility (now with rain, too), fares my modest assessment of my navigational accuracy under these particular conditions?

Two iron cylinder beacons, surmounted by red balls, showing about 15 feet above high water, one on the *Raymond* and the other on the Western Cressers, two half-tide rocks, a little within shore of the fairway line from the Mount Roads to Penzance pier, so that by keeping outside all danger is avoided.

That is satisfactory in part, but what of the hazards, if any, that lie on my immediate course to the pier?

In coming in from the eastward with a north-westerly wind (such as we are) there is, $\frac{1}{3}$ mile S-E of Penzance pier, a *rock*, called the *Gear*, which just appears at low water. There are *several sunken* rocks around it, on some of which there are no more than 3 feet. When you are turning here, take care not to shut in Little Godolphin Hill with the S.E. side of St Michael's Mount, for otherwise you will run on these rocks...

The weather is worsening fast, but another twenty minutes on this tack, and a little more on the port, should see us having cleared the rocks and off the entrance to the harbour.

Spray was enjoying herself, cleaving avidly through the grey water. She was indifferent to the sudden onslaught of heavy rain which fell upon her with a noise like rolls of drums, a noise clearly claiming superiority of status in the orchestra of sound, of wind, of pulsing white bow wave and humming shrouds that plays for us.

It is in happy abandon that *Spray* and I, seeing the basin

entrance open, the pontoon not yet having been closed, disdain the obligation to shorten sail, and approach our goal with fine finesse, over-canvassed we know, but what of it? We know we can swing through that entrance safely, in a few seconds, and we know, once through, there will be shelter in which to drop our sails in comfort, after what has turned out to be a lovely, invigorating passage.

It was getting dark when I had finished clearing things up and stowing gear away. I had a snack, and then climbed the side of the quay for a stroll. Though there was still a blustering wind, the rain had stopped, leaving a sparkle everywhere from reflections of lights on the water and wet roadway.

A town with a harbour can be, to a visitor, one of two different places depending on whether he arrives by boat or by road. He who arrives by land is a stranger, or a traveller passing through. If the latter, he makes no contact with it other than fleetingly visual; if the former he finds accommodation as best he may. In any case, his shelter will have no link with his psyche for it is but a box in which another stranger had slept the night before, and yet another one will the night following. One's feeling of identity is diminished.

But this is not so if you arrive by boat, your own floating abode. In this you bring roots with you, and when walking in the town you have a sense of belonging, have a link with the town and its people without that sense of intrusion with its element of guilt that the landlubbing visitor has.

This evening, I have tied up to the quay in the basin; the perpendicular iron ladder fixed to the wet, shining granite face is within reach. I stow away the sails, wet as they are, for the night and settle down in the cabin with a cup of coffee and a couple of biscuits. Later, I'll leave *Spray* and go to the pub nearby, but for now I stretch my legs and sit on my bunk. A good day it's been, yes, a good day.

I go over in my mind the detail, and it leads me to the reason for my being here now. Yes, Humphry Davy, the son of a woodcarver and gilder of this town of Penzance.

Before we meet him properly, just consider this scene I am

going to relate to you now: this extraordinary scene of a young man from Penzance finding himself the honoured guest of ... well, see if you don't agree with me:

From 1803 to 1815, the year that Napoleon was finally defeated by the European Powers and exiled to the island of St Helena, the Napoleonic Wars including the Peninsular War had been fought out. It was in the early stages, in 1805, that the Battle of Trafalgar was won by Nelson's fleet, a victory that put an end to Napoleon's aim to invade England.

This victory was of immense importance for it confirmed our sea supremacy and nullified the value of the huge army Napoleon had previously assembled across the English Channel for transport across to England. This army consisted of 150,000 men, the finest in the world, young in years but with ten years' experience of warfare behind them.

In England, the militia had been enrolled and volunteer corps raised throughout southern England, and elsewhere. England was kept on tenterhooks, and by the time of the Battle of Trafalgar in 1805 there were half a million men on call for national defence. It is from this anxious period in our history that the still-standing Martello towers and other measures survive to remind us of our time of peril, not to be repeated until Hitler's efforts one and a half centuries later.

I do not propose to go further into this war other than to tell enough to provide the unlikely background to the experience of our young Cornishman while it was still continuing. I will only say that in 1813, four huge armies were opposing France. They were the Prussian, the Russian and the Austrian from the east, and Wellington with the British from Spain in the south.

It was about this time that Humphry Davy was deemed worthy of an invitation from Napoleon Buonaparte to come to France and be received by him and, indeed, by the ex-Empress Josephine, too.

How could this happen at such a time, and why? Who was this man Humphry Davy? He was not in the Government, he was a private citizen, a man of science, a man of such eminence in his field that Napoleon, even at that anxious time for him, was happy for him to enter France.

It was after the Emperor had refused passports to a number of influential English noblemen that Humphry Davy, recently created a knight, attained what they had tried to do.

Napoleon was a great patron of science, and he subscribed to the view that science, like music, had no national boundaries. Thus it was that this Cornishman – whose character and achievements we shall get to know later – with his wife, and with Mr Faraday as chemical assistant, sailed from Plymouth in the middle of October and disembarked the next day at Morlaix in Brittany where they were instantly arrested by the local authorities who, quite reasonably, questioned the authenticity of their passports, believing it impossible that a party of English people could, under any circumstances, have obtained permission to travel on the Continent at a time when the only English in France were detained as prisoners.

However, after a week had passed, word came through from Paris conveying the necessary confirmation. The party was freed and allowed to proceed, arriving in Paris on the 27th of October.

Shortly after his arrival, Davy called on his old friend and associate Mr Underwood who, although one of those detained, had during the whole war enjoyed the indulgence of comparative freedom. He informed Davy that the learned members of the Institute of Science were lively in their enthusiasm for his visit.

Davy took up his abode at the Hôtel des Princes in the Rue Richelieu and it was here that Davy received these *savants*.

On 2nd November, he was received by the Imperial Institute, sitting on the right of the President, and referred to by him as 'Le Chevalier Davy'.

Lady Davy, meanwhile, intended to spend the afternoon, in the company of her maid, strolling around. They walked into the Tuileries Garden where not a very pleasing incident awaited her.

She was wearing a very small hat, of cockle-shell form such as was fashionable at the time in London. The Parisian fashion, on the other hand, was for very large bonnets. It was a Saints Day on which, the shops being closed, the Garden was filled with people taking their leisure.

On seeing the diminutive hat sported by Lady Davy, a crowd of curious spectators assembled around her, a crowd that appeared not very friendly towards this English lady.

The concourse attracted the attention of one of the wardens who informed Lady Davy that she was the object of a crowd gathering, that this could not be tolerated, and he must demand her retirement forthwith.

Some officers of the Imperial Guard to whom she appealed replied that however much they might regret the circumstances they were unable to help her.

She then asked them to conduct her to her carriage, the crowd around by now being rather frightening. An officer immediately offered his arm, but the crowd, by this time, had so greatly increased that the officer had to send for the corporal's guard. The party, with the anxious English lady in the middle, then left the Tuileries Garden with fixed bayonets.

Davy, in the event, did not meet Napoleon. More than one reason is put forward for this, the most likely being that attributed to Lady Davy to the effect that the warm reception accorded him by the *savants* of the Imperial Institute, though deeply appreciated, never influenced Davy so far as for him to forget his duty to his country as a patriot. The invitation for him to meet the Emperor at a levée, as opposed to privately, touched his sense of duty, his conscience forbidding him to take part in a levée of his country's bitterest enemy. On the other hand, it must be recorded, Davy could be both haughty and rude, and there are grounds, alas, that suggest the Emperor had heard something.

However, no such obstacles prevented him being presented to the ex-Empress at her private residence, Malmaison. He insisted on appearing for it in morning dress. It was not until after repeated efforts of persuasion, including the assurance that he would not be allowed to enter the *Salle de Reception* if he did not change his mind, that he agreed to exchange a pair of half-boots, laced in front, and which came over the lower part of his pantaloons, for a pair of black silk stockings and black leather shoes. His constantly repeated answer to the remonstrances of his friends was, 'I shall go in the same dress to Malmaison as that in which I called upon the Prince Regent at Carlton House'.

The Davys were introduced to the Ex-Empress Josephine at Malmaison. There were three English people present, one, the Earl of Beverly, in detention, another, General Sir Edward Paget, a prisoner of war, presumably 'allowed out' for the occasion, and Mr Underwood.

Let us look in on this unusual party, out of hearing of the boom of their opposing guns, but hardly according us a picture of bitter enmity.

The guests having arranged themselves in a semi-circle, the Empress enters the *Salle de Reception*, and in her usual gracious manner addresses each individual. This short ceremony being done Her Majesty retires, previously signifying to a select few her desire that they should follow her into the private apartment.

In her boudoir the conversation becomes general, covering aspects of certain works of art, Lady Davy expressing her delight at seeing some exquisite porcelain cups decorating the mantelpiece; her hostess, none other than the ex-Empress of France, presented her with one.

Lady Davy was then taken to see the conservatories which were a special pride and joy to the Empress who wanted it to be thought she possessed the finest collection of rare plants to be found in all France. Lady Davy evidently showed signs of being reluctant to take advantage of this invitation, her reason being it was a cold day and she was scantily clad.

One of the Dames du Palais sensed this and presently left the company returning, as Mr Underwood later recorded, with 'a mountain of the most costly and magnificent furs that probably had ever appeared even in a Regal Palace'.

Sir Humphry, meanwhile, was continuing to dazzle the distinguished scientists with his lectures and informal talks on his theories and discoveries which, added to his pre-visit fame as a chemist, led to him being elected to the Imperial Institute. This high honour accorded the Cornishman from Penzance was granted by forty-eight votes to one.

Now aware of the stature of Davy, while still quite young, both in England and France, I propose we turn back the pages of his career and learn something about the origins of this remarkable westcountryman.

Humphry Davy was born at Penzance on 17th December 1779. He was baptised at Penzance on 22nd January, the son of Grace Millett and Robert Davy, a wood carver who had been apprenticed to a carver in London at a time when Gibbons' work was the rage. Soon after he died the fashion for carved wood embellishments started to decline, mainly for the reason, well understood no doubt by us today, of the introduction of 'composition' (period plastic we might call it) which made things difficult for such as Robert Davy. At all events, on his return to the land of his birth he became known as the 'last of the Carvers'. He was also known as the 'Little Carver' on account of his small size. This limitation, however, did nothing to prevent his fathering a child who was to become President of the Royal Academy, and whose death was to draw from Brande, in his *History of Chemistry*, the standard work of the time, that Davy's death was no less than a 'serious national calamity'.

Lest the reader, like I felt myself, feels himself uninterested in chemistry, and in consequence, probably uninterested in Davy, I propose to present just one more appreciation of his extraordinary ability, stature of character, and, perhaps, surprisingly, poetic temperament.

A distinguished contemporary, Dr Henry, a Fellow of the Royal Society, left this appreciation for us who follow:

> Humphry Davy was bold, ardent, enthusiastic, soared to greatest heights; he commanded a wide horizon, and his keen vision penetrated to its utmost boundaries.

His imagination, in the highest degree fertile and inven-. tive, took a rapid and extensive range in analogies which he submitted to close and patient comparison with known facts tried by an appeal to ingenious and conclusive experiments.

He was imbued with the spirit, and was master in practice, of logic, and he has left us with some of the noblest examples of the efficacy of that great instrument of human reason in the discovery of truth. He applied it not only to connect classes of facts of more limited extent and importance, but to develop great and comprehensive laws, which embrace phenomena that are almost universal to the natural world.

In explaining those laws he cast upon them the illumination of his own clear and vivid conceptions; he felt an intense admiration of the beauty, harmony and order which are conspicuous in the perfect chemistry of nature; and he expressed these feelings with a force and eloquence which could issue only from a mind of the highest powers and of the finest sensibilities.

Davy's first school was the Penzance Grammar School and then, in 1793, he went to Truro where he benefited from the teaching of Dr Cardew, a man with an enviable reputation for rearing the young successfully for scholarship.

Dr Cardew had apparently not been aware that Davy's school attainment at Penzance did not measure up to the doctor's requirement, and he showed he was not anxious to retain him as a pupil in consequence. Fortunately for the boy, rejection was avoided by the doctor's recognition of Davy's potential, the quickness of his mind and his aptitude for learning.

Davy's own estimate of his educational pattern is interesting, as written in a letter some years later. Although he shows the highest respect for Dr Cardew, he considers that the comparative idleness of his time at Penzance, by allowing him to follow the bent of his own mind, favoured the development of his own special genius.

At the age of sixteen he became apprenticed to John Borlase, at that time a surgeon and apothecary, who afterwards obtained a diploma and became an eminent physician in Penzance. It was when with Borlase that he first turned his mind to the subject that was to make him famous, to chemistry. Up until then, he had developed an interest in philosophy and poetry; and the poet in him influenced his approach to his chemical studies and, later, his original experiments.

A vignette is given of Davy at this time which provides us with a sketch of him which was to develop into a large canvas of rich colours and strong, imaginative brushstrokes.

The story goes that while with Borlase it was constantly his custom to walk in the evening to Marazion to drink tea with an aunt to whom he was much attached.

On these friendly, placid visits he always took a hammer, not to use aggressively, but to procure specimens from the rocks on the beach. It could be said at the time that he paid much more attention to the bowels of the earth than the stomachs of his patients; and that when he should have been bleeding the sick, he was opening veins in granite. Instead of preparing medicines in the surgery, he was experimenting in the garret of Mr Tonkin, a family friend and his first tutor.

Mr Tonkin's garret became the centre of his experiments, but on occasions he used the doctor's surgery for them, which put all the doctor's bottles in jeopardy, the doctor, too, when a small explosion occurred.

Davy never showed interest in the surgical side of the profession, and this is indicated in a letter by a Mr Le Grice, of Penzance, who refers to this when telling an anecdote about his bathing with Davy off Battery Rocks:

> He pointed out to me a good place for diving; at the same time he talked about the tides, and Sir Isaac Newton, in a manner that greatly amazed me. I perhaps should not have so distinctly remembered him but on the following day, by my not having exactly marked the spot he had pointed out, I was nearly killed by diving on to a rock; and he came, in his

capacity of Dr Borlase's assistant, to dress the wound.

He at least had the merit of mending a broken head.

Davy had an unusual passion for oratory and often made speeches to phantom audiences. Walking along the seashore he would declaim against the howling winds and angry waves, partly with a view to overcoming a defect in his voice which, though barely noticeable when he was older, was, during his boyhood, a discordant feature.

I do not know if he declaimed his own poems on these walks, but write them he did. Indeed, Davy's popularity as a poet was not far behind his reputation as a chemist in the sense that it would be relevant for comment by any group gathered to discuss his chemistry. Southey included poems of his in the *Annual Anthology* which he edited in 1799.

At the time of his walk along the rock line of Penzance of which we have just heard, he wrote the following poem, a few verses from which I would like to quote. It is called 'The Tempest':

> The Tempest has darkened the face of the skies,
>> The winds whistle wildly across the waste plain,
> The Fiends of the whirlwind terrific arise,
>> And mingle the clouds with the white foaming main.
>
> All dark is the night, all gloomy the shore
>> Save when the red light'nings the ether divide,
> Then follows the thunder with loud-sounding roar
>> And echoes in concert the billowy tide.
>
> But though now all is murky and shaded in gloom
>> Hope, the soother, soft whispers the tempest shall cease,
> Then Nature again in her beauty shall bloom,
>> And enamour'd embrace the fair sweet smiling Peace.

At this time Davy was conducting experiments in chemistry as best he could, without the instruments and equipment he needed, and without the benefit of any experience at all, but with a pulsing enthusiasm that made up, for a while at any rate, for other deficiencies.

One of his first experiments made when he was sixteen was for the purpose of discovering the quality of air in bladders of seaweed in order to obtain results of a favourite theory of light.

Fortune was soon to favour him, for a French vessel was wrecked near Land's End, and the surgeon not only survived but eluded capture. He found his way to Penzance where Davy met him and did much to help this potential prisoner. In return for this, the surgeon presented him with a case of instruments that he had saved from the wreck, a windfall that the young chemist was to make the most of, but one that was over-shadowed at this time by perhaps the most important event in his life. This was his introduction to Mr Davies Gilbert.

Davies Gilbert was born at St Erth in 1767. He was educated at Penzance, then Pembroke College, Oxford, where he became known as the Cornish Philosopher. The latter was a fashion-able word among intellectuals at that time and could relate to engineers and chemists as well as to the discipline it refers to today.

Gilbert was a man of independent means, a man of great intellectual ability, and one to whom brilliant men like Trevithick, Faraday and Davy (as we shall see) turned to for technical and theoretical advice time and time again. He never flaunted his powers, always remaining in the background.

On leaving Oxford, Gilbert devoted his time to science, especially geology and botany, and later promoted the disciplines of science and the arts in Parliament, for he was elected Member of Parliament for Helston in 1804 and for Bodmin from 1806 to 1832.

We will see in a moment how he met Davy, but now we may ponder on the fact that this remarkable, kindly, potential genius added to his scientific and engineering mastery, the discipline of antiquarian, publishing his distinguished *Parochial History of Cornwall* in 1838.

The manner in which the meeting of the two men took place

was as curious as its result was important.

It should be said first that Davy, when a boy, presented an ungainly figure and a face that was anything that could be said to be good-looking, or even instantly attractive to anyone on first acquaintance. His figure, too, was unshapely, while his voice was thin and unappealing. Further, his presence inspired no reaction but sympathy for this shy and insignificant young man who seemed, more often than not, out of his depth with anyone but a close friend.

One day an acquaintance who happened to be walking with Mr Gilbert mentioned to him that the rather extraordinary-looking youth in question was young Davy, the carver's son who, he added, was said to be inordinately fond of making chemical experiments.

'Chemical experiments?' said Mr Gilbert. 'In that case I must have a word with him.'

Gilbert immediately perceived, on meeting and talking with Davy, that the boy revealed ample evidence of his exceptional grasp and talent, and during the ensuing week or so made occasion for a number of talks with him.

Getting to know him merely confirmed his original impression, and he offered Davy the use of his library and any other assistance that he might want in pursuit of his studies. At the same time he invited Davy to his house at Tredrea, to come as often as he wanted.

Though he was unaware of it, Davy was about to leave Penzance for the esoteric world of geniuses in the sphere of science; and before proceeding with this elevation in his studies I must mention that men of science, in general, were at this time ranged against one another so far as their adoption of one of two theories was concerned.

Not being a chemist myself, and, in the nature of things, most of my readers not very likely to be either, I am resolutely avoiding in this memoir any attempt at detail in the subjects which affected Davy, the scientist. However, there are exceptions to everything and I am now, briefly, going to outline the content of the two streams of thought whose devotees were at loggerheads.

Until the formation of the Geological Society engendered sounder views on the science, geologists, as already mentioned, were divided into two rival sects. They called themselves Neptunists or Plutonists. The former favoured the theory that the world owed its present form and arrangement exclusively to the agency of water, while the latter, conceding, to a certain extent, a role for water, maintained the utter impossibility of explaining the consolidation of the strata without the intervention of fire.

Geologists felt bound to side with one or the other of these contending theories, for neutrality was considered reprehensible. The professors of Oxford and Cambridge kept the fire of controversy well and truly alight by taking opposite sides. Two of these contending professors were Beddoes and Hailstone. Doctor Beddoes was a violent and uncompromising Plutonist, while Hailstone was an emphatic Neptunist.

Cornwall had a place in this vociferous argument as it was thought that the rocks there, with their granitic veins, might afford evidence upon the subject. The two professors were good friends, agreeing to differ, so that it is not surprising they decided to journey together to this field of dispute, each hoping he would prove to be victor.

In due course, the two belligerents appeared at Penzance in company with Davies Gilbert; but in spite of earnest attempts at approaching the problem in an air of amiable neutrality, each tackled the examination of the rocks in the human way of choosing samples most suitable in support of their own theory and ignoring the rest. One protested that the very aspect of the shivered slate was sufficient to prove that the globe must have been roasted, the other, with equal plausibility, declared there was not a tittle of evidence to show that the watery solvent had ever even simmered.

Doctor Beddoes had recently established in Bristol what was called the Pneumatic Institution which he founded for the purpose of investigating further the nature of gases, and the application of their ingredients to possible remedial purposes for illnesses.

At the time of his visit to Penzance, Doctor Beddoes was on the look-out for an assistant at this Institution and his eye fell on this rather uncouth young man of nineteen years, Humphry Davy, the Cornish lad whom Davies Gilbert had brought to his attention as a natural chemist of great promise.

The events and opinions that led up to this possibility are outlined in letters written at the time.

In a note appended later to Davy's paper subsequently published in the first volume of *West Country Contributions*, Doctor Beddoes writes, 'My first knowledge of Mr Davy arose from a letter written in April 1798, containing an account of his researches on Heat and Light.' The rest is told in letters passed between Doctor Beddoes and Mr Gilbert of which the following are extracts:

In a letter dated 4th July 1798, Beddoes says:

I am glad that Mr Davy has impressed you as he has me. I have long wished to write to you about him, for I think he can open a more fruitful field of investigation than anybody else. Is it not also his most direct road to fortune? Should he not bring out a favourable result, he may still exhibit his talents for investigation, and entitle himself to public confidence more effectually than by any other mode. He must be maintained, but the [Institution's] fund will not furnish a salary from which a man can lay up anything. He must also devote his time for two or three years to the investigation. I wish you would converse with him upon the subject. I am sorry I cannot specify a yearly sum, nor can I say with certainty whether all the subscribers will accede to the plan. I have written to the principal ones, and will lose no time in sounding them all.

As one would expect, Davy took his position with the Pneumatic Institution very seriously, contriving new forms of laboratory equipment which could fulfil the ideas he had for the search for healing properties of inhaled gas.

It could not be expected for laymen such as ourselves to

fathom the detail of these chemical experiments; but the whole embraces in some measure our own experience, and it is this, with nitrous oxide gas, that we will follow from Davy's own account. It illustrates the lengths to which he would expose himself to risk for the sake of the scientist's search for the key to unlock the secret cells of nature.

In April 1800, Davy achieved the isolation of nitrous oxide in a state of purity, discovering many of its chemical properties in the process. Reflections on these properties made him resolve to 'inspire' (breathe it in) it in its true form. He could see no other way in which its benefits might be used to help a patient other than by inhaling it.

He was aware of the danger of the experiment and he thought that the effects might be depressing and painful. There were, however, a number of reasons that made him believe that a single inspiration of gas, apparently possessing no immediate action on the irritable fibre [of the lungs], could not endanger his life.

On 11th April he made the first inspiration of pure nitrous oxide. It passed through the bronchial tubes and produced no uneasy sensation in the lungs. The result of this experiment induced him to believe that breathing it in was not likely to prove harmful. Accordingly, he deemed it safe to make a further experiment, and on 16th April he repeated it. On this occasion, not by Davy's design, Doctor Kirkdale was present.

Davy breathed in three quarts of nitrous oxide from, and into, a silk bag, for more than half a minute, and without previously closing his nose or exhausting his lungs. The first inhalations caused a slight feeling of giddiness, which was followed by a feeling of pressure in his head, accompanied by a blurring of sensation and willpower, rather like the feeling produced in the first stages of intoxication. It was not a pleasant feeling.

This trial failed to satisfy him, and when comparing it with the former ones he could not decide whether it was stimulating or depressing.

He related this to Doctor Beddoes who, on 17th April, was

present at a further experiment. Having previously blocked his nostrils and emptied his lungs of air, Davy breathed four quarts of the gas from, and into, a silk bag. His first feelings were similar to those of the last experiment; but in less than half a minute, the inhaling being continued, they became diminished gradually, and were succeeded by a sensation analogous to gentle pressure on all the muscles, attended by a highly pleasurable thrilling, particularly in the chest and in the extremities.

The objects around him appeared dazzling, and his hearing more acute. Towards the end, the thrilling increased, the sense of muscular power became stronger, and at last, an irresistible urge to action was indulged in, his movements of his limbs being various and violent. These effects soon ceased, once the gas was turned off, and after ten minutes he had regained his natural state of mind. However, the thrilling at his extremities continued longer.

This experiment was conducted in the morning. No languor or exhaustion resulted; his feelings throughout the day were as usual, and he had a good night.

The courage of Davy in undertaking such experiments is to be admired and wondered at. Knowing very well the risks he was taking, his eagerness to break through to success led him to defy permanent injury; and he was not lacking physical warnings.

For 'eagerness' as I have put it, Davy called it enthusiasm. For instance, he wrote of an ensuing experience:

...I transferred my lips from the mouthpiece of the bag to that of the air-holder, and, turning the stopcock, attempted to [breathe in] the nitrous gas. In passing through my mouth it tasted astringent and highly disagreeable: it occasioned a sense of burning in the throat, and produced a spasm of the epiglottis, so painful as to oblige me to desist immediately from attempts to inhale it. After removing my lips from the mouthpiece, when I opened them to breathe common air, *nitrous acid* was immediately formed in my mouth which

burnt the tongue and palate, injured the teeth, and produced
an inflammation of the mucous membrane which lasted for
some hours.

A further experiment, this time inhaling hydro-carbonate
instead of nitrous oxide, had a frightening effect. I give here
Davy's urbane account of it in a paper, *Researches* (*1800*), nearly
two centuries later, as a tribute to the kind of sacrifice this scion
of Penzance was voluntarily involved in for the sake of medical
progress.

The first inhalation of the gas

produced a sort of numbness and loss of feeling in the chest
and about the pectoral muscles. After the second I lost all
power of perceiving external things and had no distinct
sensation, except that of a terrible oppression on the chest.
During the third exhalation this feeling subsided, I seemed
sinking into annihilation, and just power enough to cast off
the mouthpiece from my unclosed lips.

A short interval must have passed during which I breathed
common air, before the objects around me became dis-
tinguishable. On recollecting myself, I faintly articulated, 'I
do not think I shall die'.

Placing my finger on the wrist, I found my pulse threadlike
and beating with excessive quickness. In less than a minute I
was able to walk, and the painful oppression on the chest
directed me to the open air.

After making a few steps that carried me to the garden, my
head became giddy, and I had just enough voluntary power
to throw myself on the grass. Here the painful feeling of the
chest increased with such violence as to threaten suffocation.

At this moment I asked for some nitrous oxide. Mr Dwyer
brought me a mixture of this gas with oxygen and I breathed
it for a minute and believed myself recovered.

In five minutes painful feelings began gradually to
diminish; in an hour they had nearly disappeared and I felt
only excessive weakness and a slight swimming in the head.

My voice was very feeble and indistinct.

I afterwards walked slowly for half an hour with Mr Tonkin and on my return was so much stronger and better as to believe the effects of the gas entirely passed off, though my pulse was 120 and very feeble. I continued without pain for nearly three quarters of an hour, when the giddiness returned with such violence as to oblige me to lie on the bed; it was accompanied with nausea, loss of memory, and deficient sensation.

In about an hour and a half the giddiness went off and was replaced by an excruciating pain in the forehead and between the eyes, with transient pains in the chest and the extremities.

Towards night these affections gradually diminished; and at ten no disagreeable feeling, except weakness, remained. I slept sound and in the morning very feeble and very hungry. No recurrence of the symptoms took place and I had nearly regained my strength by the evening.

I have been minute in the account of this experiment because it proves that hydro-carbonate acts as a sedative; that is, it produces diminution of vital action, and consequent debility, without previously exciting. There is every reason to believe that, had I taken four or five inhalations, instead of three, they would have destroyed life immediately, without producing any painful sensation.

With dismay, some may think it was relevant that Davy was to die at the early age of fifty-one.

Knowing little about chemistry as I do, it is not my intention, as I have already indicated, to make this memoir the story of the chemist, but, rather, the story of the man, though the light from his brilliance as a scientist shines vividly through the technical shadows that we cannot understand and onto his character and influence on the world of science.

His influence impinged on the world of letters and poetry, too; and I have not introduced the reader to his friends, such famous poets as Coleridge and Southey, who had the greatest admiration for Davy not only as a friend, but as a poet, an aspect of his virtues that often served to help fashion imaginative experiments that a more mundane scientist, however brilliant, would never perceive.

Hear what two of these distinguished men of letters thought of Davy. First Coleridge:

> There is an energy and elasticity in Davy's mind which enables him to seize on and analyse all questions, pushing them to their legitimate consequences. Every subject in Davy's mind has the principle of vitality – living thoughts spring up, like the turf under his feet.

And Southey comments:

> Davy is proceeding in his chemical career with the same giant strides as at his outset. His book upon the nitrous oxide will form an epoch in the science. I never witnessed such indefatigable activity in any other man, nor ardour so regulated by cool judgement.

While he was superintending the Pneumatic Institution in Clifton (Bristol), Davy's notes on his experiments were mingled with more philosophical ideas, with reflections, with resolutions and with bold ideas and programmes for his future labours. His brother, Doctor Davy, has left us in his *Life* of his brother a glimpse of his mode of living by quoting an extract from these notes of his pattern of work.

Writing in 1799, while living in a house he had taken in Dowry Square, Clifton, he spent two hours before breakfast reading. The five hours from nine to two were given to experiments, from four to six to reading, and from seven to ten pm to the study of metaphysics.

The time was passed happily at Clifton in pleasing activity with sympathetic friends and with a good enough salary to cover not only his own needs but also to assist his mother and his brother's education in Penzance.

After little more than eighteen months, the prospect of a new appointment of singular importance was put before him by the President of the Royal Institution, Count Rumford: it was to engage him as lecturer. The account of events at this time is happily told in a letter Davy wrote to his friend and sponsor, Davies Gilbert, and headed 8th March, 1801.

'I cannot think of quitting the Pneumatic Institution,' he writes, 'without giving you intimation of it in a letter; indeed, I believe I should have done this some time ago had not the hurry of business and the fever of emotion produced by the prospect of novel changes in futurity, destroyed to certain extent my powers of consistent action.' After further expressions of concern and gratitude, Davy goes on to tell Gilbert what has been happening.

Some four weeks before, he had received an invitation to go to London to attend on Count Rumford who had some proposals to make relative to the Royal Institution. There, after several discussions he was invited by the Managers of the Institution to become the Director of their laboratory and Assistant Professor of Chemistry. Salary, and conditions, were satisfactory but far more important for Davy was the provision 'that he would have the sole and uncontrolled use of the apparatus of the Institution, and the provision of any apparatus he might need for new experiments ...'.

The first notice of Davy's name in the Minute Book of the Royal Institution occurs in the Report adopted at a Meeting of the Managers on Monday, 16th February 1801. In it is recorded his engagement in the capacity of Assistant Lecturer in Chemistry, Director of, and Assistant Editor of the Institution Journals. Included in the contract is the provision of a room in the house and free coals and free supply of candles. His salary was to be one hundred guineas per annum.

A month later, on 16th March, the Minutes record that a room had been prepared for Mr Davy and that he had arrived at the Institution on the 15th March.

I have had occasion to refer to the rather uncouth manner that Davy sported. Count Rumford apparently was not too adversely struck by this during the series of meetings he had had with the young chemist prior to his appointment.

However, the first impression of Count Rumford of the personal appearance of the new addition to the staff once he had arrived was highly unfavourable. He told Mr Underwood (a gentleman ardently attached to science and devoted to the Royal Institution) of his great regret at having been influenced by 'the ardour with which his suit had been urged'. Davy's first lecture, however, entirely removed every objection and immediately resulted in him being given the large theatre in which to lecture.

Throughout his early youth, Davy had suffered, from a social point of view, a handicap in manner which he unconsciously tried to disclaim by being boorish and unattractively assertive. This showed, too, in a pertness of manner, and in a smirk on his face that was not calculated to make friends. But from this time onward, with the self-esteem his appointment with the Royal Institution engendered, things became much better for him.

At a meeting of Managers held in July it was decided that a course of lectures on the Chemical Principles of the Art of Tanning should be given by Davy beginning on 2nd November, and he was given leave of absence, as required, during the months of July, August and September in order to make himself particularly acquainted with the practical part of the business of tanning.

During this period he found it expedient to go down to Cornwall. Joining him as companion was Mr Underwood. They arrived at Penzance staying with his mother, and from there walked along the edge of the cliffs round Land's End, Cape Cornwall, St Just, and from St Ives to Redruth and back to Penzance.

Two days later they set off again and trudged along the shore to the Lizard. Mr Underwood was delighted. In his Journal he wrote:

Kynance Cove had from the commencement of our intimacy been a daily theme of his conversation. No epithets were sufficiently forcible to express his admiration at the beauty of the spot, the enthusiastic delight with which he dwelt upon the description of the Serpentine rocks, polished by the waves and reflecting the brightest tints from their surfaces, seemed inexhaustible, and when we arrived at the spot he appeared absolutely entranced.

During these excursions his conversation was most romantic and poetical. His views of Nature and her sublime operations, were expressed without reserve as they rapidly presented themselves to his imagination; they were the ravings of genius, but even his nonsense was that of a superior being.

For the next few years there was a boundless series of successes for the Cornish boy, now not in the least abashed by the sophistication of the world of high society, of the rarest of atmospheres in which his fellow academics lived and in the glory of the light of success that followed him everywhere.

But then, an embarrassing hiccough for him occurred, and loud enough for it to be heard far and wide in a manner that caused him much embarrassment.

And what was it? In the month of August 1811, he was asked to look into the ventilation system in the House of Lords in which was much to be desired. This he did, but with devastating results. Whether he had miscalculated the diameter and number of apertures necessary for obtaining an improved current of air is difficult to say. There was, however, no difficulty in recognising that it was an abysmal failure. Needless to say the debacle was a grand opportunity for envious colleagues, and others, to make fun of this non-achievement by the great Davy, and Davy did not take it easily.

However, the shadow was soon eliminated by really good news. The Prince Regent, desiring to add his tribute to the public acclaim of Davy's achievements and talent, bestowed the honour of knighthood upon him at a levée held at Carlton House on Wednesday, 18th April 1812. He was only thirty-four years old. The carver's son from Penzance had come far. This event was followed, only four days later, by an even greater event, for the new knight took unto himself in marriage a wealthy widow of good family, bringing with her a passport into realms of social importance which, by now, Davy had shown increasing signs of being influenced by (in the nicest possible way).

The bride was Jane Apreece, the widow of Sir John Sebright Apreece, and a lady of very considerable fortune in her own right, being the daughter and heiress of Charles Kerr of Kelso.

On the day following the marriage, Sir Humphry delivered his farewell address to the Royal Institution. During their honeymoon in Scotland, Davy wrote several letters to his scientific friends and others. To his mother he described her as a 'woman equally distinguished for virtues, talents and accomplishments'; and to his brother as the 'most amiable and intellectual woman I have ever known'.

And here is a pleasing homely picture of Lady Davy as recounted in the *Life of George Ticknor*, a contemporary:

15 June – As her husband invited me to do, I called this morning on Lady Davy. I found her in her parlour working on a dress, the contents of her basket strewed about the table, and looking more like home than anything since I left it. She is small with black eyes and hair, a very pleasant face and a pleasing smile; and when she speaks has much spirit and expression in her countenance.

Life proceeded happily for the couple, now ensconced in a fine house, 28 Lower Grosvenor Street, London. To this comfortable domestic background he built a career that brought the fame of this Cornishman's talents to every country in Europe: as poet, philosopher and chemist extraordinary he was acclaimed, his talents in his own country being recognised by such honours as the Presidency of the Royal Society and his promotion by the King to a baronetcy. In Appendix B, the reader who wants to dig deeper into the professional side of Davy's activities will find details of subjects about which he lectured, reported on and wrote papers on.

We are now approaching a period of intensive activity on Davy's part, of a kind that was to save lives, of an apparatus that he devised which, essentially the same today as then, still shields workers from an ever-present danger. On 9th September he delivered before the Royal Society one of his most important papers. It arose from a catastrophe.

On 25th May 1812, there had taken place at Felling Colliery, Sunderland, an appalling accident that was all the more shocking because the equipment and efficiency of the mine was considered one of the finest, if not *the* finest, in the country.

At about half-past eleven in the morning, the neighbouring villages were alarmed by a tremendous explosion. A subterranean fire swept along a gallery and up two of the shafts. For half a mile around a slight trembling was felt as from an earthquake, and the noise of the explosion, though dull, was heard up to three or four miles away.

Immense quantities of dust and small coal accompanied these blasts. They rose high into the air like an inverted cone. The heaviest part of the ejected coal and rubble and timber fell near the pit, but the dust, borne away by a strong west wind, fell in a continuous shower for a distance of a mile and a half. In the village of Haworth it caused a gloom like that of early twilight, and so covered the roads that shoes left imprints in it.

Wives and children of the pitmen rushed to the working pit, and every face showed terror at this ghastly visitation, incredulity at what was happening. By twelve o'clock, thirty-two survivors had been brought to the surface. The dead bodies of two boys, miserably scorched and shattered were brought up at the same time.

Let us take a look at the background that led to this disaster, one that was to inspire Davy to concentrate his powers in developing his miner's lamp: for let it be remembered that there was no electricity for centuries of coal-mining history, only the naked flame lighting the workings in the coal mine.

The galleries and shafts of the coalfield in which Felling Colliery lay amounted to some forty miles in length. Miners might have to walk them for forty minutes from their shaft before they reached their dark, cramped or cavernous workings. Ventilation was often inadequate allowing fire damp (the mixture of oxygen and coaldust) to gather, offering always a potential fire bomb to develop, as though the whole mine were a magazine.

On the approach of a candle the expanding 'gas' drove all before it as though there was a roaring whirlwind of flaming air which tore up everything in its progress, scorching some of the miners to a cinder, and burying others under enormous ruins shaken from the roof.

A contemporary writer indicates the pressure that Davy must have felt to use his talents to achieve a solution ...

To collect and publish a detailed account of the numerous and awful accidents which have occurred in the last few years, from the explosion of inflammable air, or *fire-damp*, would present a picture of the most appalling nature. In the space of seven years upwards of three hundred pitmen had been suddenly deprived of their lives, their women and children left in a state of the greatest distress and poverty ...

Some time later – over a year, in fact – a society was formed with the name 'Society for Preventing Accidents in Coal-Mines'. One of the distinguished sponsors was Sir Ralph Milbanke, a coal-owner, in one of whose mines there was a very bad accident, with twenty-seven dead, only a few days before the first meeting.

One of the sponsors, the Reverend Dr Gray, got in touch with Davy inviting him to consider helping them in their search for a remedy to reduce the awful accidents. Davy agreed to help and forthwith obtained supplies of various specimens of fire-damp for analysis.

In less than a fortnight, he was writing good news to Dr Gray:

Royal Institution Oct. 30

My dear Sir,

As it was the consequence of your invitation that I endeavoured to investigate the nature of the fire-damp, I owe to you the first notice of the progress of my experiments.

My results have been successful far beyond my expectations. I shall enclose a little sketch of my views upon the subject ...

Only six weeks later, Davy was able to write the following to Dr Gray:

Grosvenor Street, December 15

My dear Sir,

...... I shall enclose the first sheet of my paper [being prepared for the Royal Society] and shall be glad to preface it by some observations when you print it.

I shall forward my lanterns and lamps to you in a few days. They are *absolutely safe*: and if the miners have any more explosions it will be their own fault.

You will find, when you see my construction, that the principles as well as the execution are entirely new.

I am, my dear Sir, very sincerely yours,

H. Davy.

Towards the end of his life, Humphry Davy devoted much effort to finding a means of prevention of erosion of the copper sheathing covering the hulls of vessels by the sea. This was a task undertaken at the request of the Government.

To some extent he was successful in this endeavour by coating the copper with tin, but though the tin prevented the erosion of the copper, it did not prevent the fouling of the metal by accretions of seaweed and shells, so the one advantage cancelled out the other.

Davy took this failure very badly, and became in some respects a different man. The disappointment came at a time his health was failing. As time went on he remained unsettled and withdrawn, over-sensitive to any criticism. The death of his mother affected him further.

On St Andrew's Day 1826, he gave what proved to be his last Address to the Royal Society, and shortly afterward suffered a slight stroke. During his recovery he made his Will which included £100, the interest from which 'may be annually paid to the Master of Penzance Grammar School, on condition that the boys may have a holiday on his birthday'.

Davy spent some months in Rome, and then, with Lady Davy and his brother, Doctor Davy, took up his abode at the Hôtel de la Couronne in Geneva. They arrived at four o'clock, and he later dined, eating heartily and joking with the waiter about the way the fish had been cooked. He would like, he told him, during his stay at the hotel, to be served with every possible variety of fish that the Lake of Geneva provided.

Davy had a cup of tea before going to bed. He settled down for the night at midnight. His servant, who slept in a bed alongside him in the same alcove, was almost immediately told to fetch his brother.

On Doctor Davy entering his room he said, 'I am dying' or words to that effect. He went on, 'And when it is all over, I desire that no disturbance of any kind be made in the house. Lock the door, and let everyone retire to his apartment.'

At about a quarter to three, on 29th May 1829, Sir Humphry Davy of Penzance, died in peace. He was buried in Geneva.

*

There is an intriguing postscript to this visit of ours in *Spray* to Penzance.

It is the following morning. All signs of rain have gone, and instead there is an optimistic feel in the air, with modest cumulus clouds skimming across the patchwork blue and white and grey of sky.

Spray is swanning happily along, before a stiff following breeze, across Mount's Bay, toward the Lizard and the east. Her motion is easy, languid in the following swell. She sways slightly from side to side, up and down, giving time for me to look around and about and enjoy the scenery.

And now, quite suddenly my mind is assailed by a thrilling concept embracing coincidence with pride, wonder with humility.

I look across the water. Within the perimeter of Mount's Bay, from Penzance to the fishing village of Porthleven, and Helston a mile inland beyond it, there were born, at the end of the eighteenth century, two men whose inventions were destined to have worldwide significance in terms of the saving of lives.

These two were Henry Trengrouse and Humphry Davy. We have already met Humphry Davy and some of my readers may have met Trengrouse, of Helston, in my *Cornwall and the Tumbling Sea*. He it was who invented the rocket apparatus that lifts shipwrecked crew from wreck to shore or wreck to clifftop; and about Davy's merciful invention of the coalminers' safety lamp we know already.

Thousands and thousands of lives have been saved by these two inventions of two local Cornishmen, the one being the son of a woodcarver, and the other, strangely enough, also from 'wood' stock, being the son of a cabinet-maker.

Their inventions are in use all over the world, yet the inventors were born within six miles of one another and within six years.

Surely, a flash of concentrated talent in a timeless world.

V

Admiral Exmouth, yet Cornish

I find it always a solemn experience sailing past Lizard Point, no matter how friendly and sublime the weather might be.

Today, all is in *Spray's* favour as we sail eastwards along the Lizard coastline a mile away to port. It is a bold, high, massive *i* lump of land with vicious outcrops of rock, whence a light for seamen, of some sort, has spelled a warning and shone its guiding identification for vessels for the last three hundred years.

The Lizard is often the landfall for ships reaching home waters after voyages from halfway across the world. Countless ships' captains, denied the weather to get a sun sight or other celestial observation for days, and forced to rely only on dead-reckoning to get safely into the relatively narrow entrance into the Channel, have rejoiced when the bold contour of the Lizard has showed up and their true position made known.

But other vessels, many others, approaching in weather conditions that make the Lizard change from an angel into a demon, have seen it too late and have endured the agony of a relentless combination of wind and tide, and have joined the rocky tombs of those who preceded them, engulfed by the power of the sea.

Casualties have tended to be more spectacular there than anywhere else as so many passenger liners and large cargo vessels have passed the Lizard on their lawful occasions.

For some eighty years it was from here that the coastguards provided Lloyds, of London, with the list of passing ships. This famous 'Lloyds List' appeared daily in *The Times* and many other newspapers. As Cyril Noall puts it in his book

Cornish Lights and Shipwrecks, more than 1,500 vessels pass the Point in the course of a month, and to each of them the twin white buildings of today which include the lighthouse, or the flashing beam by night, bid welcome or farewell to the shores of England.

A few years back, before the days when yachts became similar to sea-going offices complete with telephones, *Spray* and I were on our way from Falmouth to Cork. It was quite rough before the coastguard station was abeam to starboard, some two miles inshore.

My system then for communicating my report to the Lizard Signals Station was by flashing it in morse with an Aldis lamp.

With one arm hooked around the mast and resting the heavy lamp in the crook of the other, swaying against the varied and rapid movements of *Spray*, I put my eye to the telescopic sight and trained it as best I could on the Station.

I flashed: *Spray of Glendorgal from Falmouth for Cork.*

The station asked for a repeat, then signalled: *Understood.* A momentary link with terra firma was cut, and we were on our own again. Some days later I saw *The Times* of the following day. The report from Lloyds Station of ships sighted from the Lizard included the names of thirteen vessels. Among those thirteen, printed next to one another, were *Queen Elizabeth II* and *Spray of Glendorgal.*

So be it, the whale and the minnow on equal terms, with the restless sea and the winds their common birthright.

There is no grand ship in view today, but allow one's imagination some rein and there is no lack of ships to see on their lawful, and unlawful, occasions in these waters off the Lizard. Once the time barrier is removed from my consciousness, I can see the fleets of ships on these waters that link us to them. What I see from *Spray* now is precisely the same as, say, a Cornishman called Edward Pellew saw it two hundred years ago.

He was a naval captain who, though a fine officer and seaman, left the Navy for two main reasons, one because he was bored by the fact there had been no war for years, and two, because the needs of his increasing family outstripped the pay he was getting in the Navy. He and his brother, also in the Navy, decided to farm at Treverry, near Falmouth, and being inexperienced failed entirely to gain the revenue they had hoped for.

Fate came to Edward fortuitously in the form of a war. At the beginning of 1793 there had been no suggestion of hostilities, but then came the French Revolution and, quite unexpectedly, war was declared on England twelve days after the death of the French King, Louis XVI.

The Government had made no preparation for such an event, and were taken completely by surprise, as was the country as a whole. The Navy was on peace establishment with only sixteen thousand seamen and marines, a paltry complement compared to the sixty thousand it was found necessary to raise during the course of the year.

Immediately they heard of this, the Pellew brothers sped to London. Edward was forthwith appointed to the *Nymphe*, 36 guns, formerly a French frigate and taken by boarding in the former war after having had her steering disabled.

As soon as he received his appointment, Edward set about, as captain, the task of manning her as quickly as possible. His brother had returned to Falmouth, so it was to him he wrote urgently, asking him to recruit men for crew, sailors if possible, but if that were not possible, then *Cornish miners*.

The choice at first sight may seem odd but he thought, quite rightly as it turned out, that the miners were likely to make better seamen than any other class of landsman, and it was a time when many were out of work with families short of food.

There were, too, Pellew perceived, certain important similarities in the work of miner and seaman. Both were familiar with the use of ropes as a central facility in their work, both were accustomed to climb difficult surfaces, both were familiar with the use of gunpowder, and both seamen and miners often found themselves in a situation where they were alone in coping with it, thus they were frequently acting on their own judgement.

This employment of miners in the Navy had never been done before, but they soon showed their superiority over the average landsman who had the misfortune to be caught by the press gang and thrust as an innocent into the tough environment of a heaving ship of war at sea.

Industry in Cornwall was confined to the mines and fishery, agriculture being neglected so that the country was dependent on the import of agricultural products and famine was not uncommon.

At such times the tinners would crowd into the towns or wherever they believed that corn was stored, with their bags and what money they had, and demand that food should be provided for them at a price they could afford. Violence sometimes erupted, but on the whole, though the law condemned such happenings, sympathy with them, in general, was apparent.

During one of these periods of distress when there was a great quantity of corn in the customs-house cellars at Falmouth, a strong body of miners came threateningly to be supplied with some of it. But the occasion exemplified the basic sense of law and order of the Cornish miner for though they were famished, as one account put it, they listened to Mr Pellew, the Collector (a relation to Edward), as he explained to them why he had no powers to sell it, and they agreed to leave the town peaceably.

In the event, eighty miners volunteered and made the journey up to Spithead where they joined the frigate *Nymphe*. She sailed to Falmouth, still undermanned, the passage proving a good exercise for the eighty Cornish novices, who had to learn fast for there were only eleven professional seamen.

One wonders whether these volunteers from the mines in Cornwall had any idea of the kind of life that existed on board a man-of-war. At the time of which we speak, namely, the French Revolutionary War, February 1793, the enemy fleet was formidable, and the English Channel was a lively place to patrol in. Our miners, therefore, would be in no doubt that they would meet with action; but did they have any idea at all of what it was like to be a member of a gun's crew in action against the enemy? I doubt it, and as only very few of my readers are likely to be any less ignorant, I have included a personal account by a naval officer of his personal view of an action in this same period. It comes from *Scenes and Adventures in the Life of Mildmay*, and you will see it as Appendix C. So turn, dear reader, to that now, if you feel strong enough to have your eyes opened.

The *Nymphe* did not have to wait long before she was in action. She was first engaged in escorting convoys, one from Falmouth to the Nore, another from the Nore to Hamburg and another from Cuxhaven to the Nore again.

From the Nore she returned to Spithead and now joined company with the *Venus*, Captain Faulknor. Not one of her crew had yet seen a shot fired, but Israel, Edward Pellew's brother, had joined her, much to his brother's delight.

On 27th May, the *Venus* had engaged a French frigate, *Cleopatra*, one of a squadron then patrolling in the Channel. She was under the orders of a very experienced French officer, Captain Millon, and in due course she met up with the *Nymphe*. The ship was more fully manned now, for Captain Pellew had taken her into Falmouth, and there 'pressed' the crew of a South Seas vessel. 'Pressing', the name given to the work of the more familiar press gang, was the only way the Navy could man its ships. It was a horrible activity whereby a man could be picked up almost anywhere and whisked off and forced into the Navy: for what could be many years. I always feel the most brutal occasion for it was when a merchant vessel was approaching port after a voyage, perhaps, of two years duration. The press gang boat would be ready to intercept it and then would go alongside and literally haul off however many men they wanted; and that would be the end of the dreams nurtured aboard by the home-coming seamen. Instead of home, of being reunited with loved ones, those pressed would be abruptly taken off, put as crew in a man-of-war, and be off again to sea, perhaps for another two or three years having had no contact with home.

I direct myself, for a moment now, to any of my readers who imagine they are not interested in the sea or fighting ships. I urge them not only to bear with me, but join me, free of prejudice, as I give them the opportunity to share in an engagement between two frigates of the British Navy and the enemy, at the outset of the Navy's long and brilliant achievement of being Mistress of the Seas.

At daybreak, on 19th June 1793, the *Nymphe* was sailing up Channel some miles to the westward of Start Point when a sail to the south-east caught the captain's attention, and it was not long before he was sure it was a French frigate.

By six o'clock they had closed, with the enemy making no attempt to escape. Shortly the vessel was confirmed as being the *Cleopatra*, and Pellew knew that she would be in good shape with a well-trained crew under Captain Millon.

Such a challenge was very provocative for Pellew, and he made ready to fight. The ships were now so near that sombre greetings could be exchanged by the two crews as was the custom. The two captains, each standing on their poop, hailed one another. Not a shot was fired. The crew of the *Nymphe* (who knows, perhaps to the bewilderment of the eighty Cornish miners?) now shouted 'Long live King George!' followed by three hearty cheers.

Captain Millon was then seen to address his crew briefly, holding in his hand a 'cap of liberty' which he waved before them.

They answered by shouting, 'Vive la République!' The symbol, the cap of liberty, was then given to a sailor who ran up the shrouds of the mainmast and fixed it to the masthead.

At a quarter past six, the *Nymphe* had closed to a position off the starboard quarter of the *Cleopatra* when Pellew, who had been bareheaded, raised his hat to his head which was the pre-arranged signal for his ship to open fire.

Each frigate started a furious exchange of fire which carried on violently for some three-quarters of an hour to a contrasting background of blue sea and modest westerly breeze, and sometimes the two vessels would come very close to one another.

At a little before seven (still in the morning) the mizzenmast of the *Cleopatra* was hit, and shortly after the wheel was shot away. Now rendered unmanageable, she swung round toward the *Nymphe* and collided, her long jib boom pressing hard against the mainmast.

Imagining that the enemy was going to board, Captain Pellew ordered his own boarders up on deck to repel them in hand to hand fighting. However, he soon realised that *Cleopatra* was out of control, so that it was the *Nymphe* who became the attacker, and her boarders jumped onto *Cleopatra's* fo'c'stle, a division of them also boarding through the maindeck gun ports and fighting their way through the bewildered gunners and up onto the quarterdeck.

The surprise of the attack, and its ferocity, were too much for the enemy and they fled down below and gave in, their pendant being hauled down in surrender. The two vessels were now locked together by the masts and rigging of each of the heaving ships being entwined with one another, and meanwhile fighting was continuing between-decks, surely a horrifying experience for those involved.

Fortunately, the jib-boom suddenly snapped and this had the effect of freeing somewhat the rigging confusion, but still it held the two ships together. Captain Pellew could see that perhaps it could be cleared if a man went aloft with a knife, so he called for a volunteer to climb up and go out on the main topsail yard, high above the rolling decks, promising him ten guineas if he succeeded.

And still bloody, hand-to-hand fighting continued below decks; but then, suddenly, the two ships fell apart, the enemy ship, now a prize, falling astern, but not before half the prisoners had been transferred to the *Nymphe*.

Pellew's inexperienced crew, the composition of which, as we have seen, comprised few professionals, had fought gallantly. One boy, who had served previously in only one ship, the *Winchelsea*, and that as a barber's boy, was made second captain of one of the big main-deck guns. The captain being killed, he became its captain. Throughout the rest of the action, Captain Pellew heard him from the gangway give the word for all the successive steps of loading as calmly as if they had been at exercise.

In the heat of the action, an action steeped in the nightmarish noise of explosions, of shouts and screams, of splintering wood and grinding hulls, of acrid smoke and blood and bones, one of the men came from the main deck to ask the Captain what he must do as all the men at his gun were killed or wounded but himself, and he had been trying to fight it alone, but could not.

Another, who had joined only the day before, was found seated on a gun-carriage complaining that he had been very well as long as he was fighting but that he felt bad as soon as it was over, and that he did not know what was the matter with his leg it was smarting so much. It was found that the poor fellow had a musket ball in it.

The loss, on both sides, was severe, and nearly equal in proportion to the two crews. The *Nymphe*, out of a crew of 240, had 23 killed and 27 wounded, while the *Cleopatra* had 63 killed out of a crew of 320.

Captain Millon, the captain of the *Cleopatra*, was killed. A cannon-shot struck him in the back carrying away much of his left hip. The story goes that despite this frightful wound, the dying man did not forget the importance of destroying his code list, but, in his agony, he took out of his pocket his commission as Captain of the *Cleopatra*, and he died actually swallowing it. This code, so valuable as long as the enemy did not know it to be in the hands of the British, thus fell into those of Pellew who later despatched it to the Admiralty.

On the following day the gallant captain sailed his prize into Portsmouth harbour. He sent the flag under which he fought to his elder brother, Sam, in Cornwall.

He also sent to Sam that curious emblem, the 'cap of liberty' already mentioned, which I now discover was about seven inches long, made of wood and painted red, with a round tapering spear of brass about three and a half feet long. The lower half of this was blackened with a screw arrangement at the end to fix it to the mast. This capture of it by Captain Pellew was recognised as being the first trophy of this nature taken in the revolutionary war.

Edward Pellew, at the same time, sent Sam (Collector of Customs at Falmouth), a concise description of events. Here it is:

Dear Sam, – Here we are – thank God! safe – after a glorious action with *la Cleopatre*, the crack ship of France; 40 guns, 28 on her main deck and 12 on her quarter-deck, some of 36 pounds [weight of cannon ball], and 320 men. We dished her up in fifty minutes, boarded, and struck her colours.

We have suffered much, but I was long determined to make a short affair of it. We conversed before we fired a shot, and then, God knows, hot enough it was ... I might have wrote for a month had I entered on the description of every gallant action, but we were all in it, heart and soul. I owe much to Israel who undertook with the after-gun to cut off her rudder and wheel. The tiller was shot away, and four men were killed at her wheel, which I verily believe was owing to him.

I will write again in a day or two, and do all I can for everybody. We must go into harbour. *Cleopatra* is fifteen feet longer, and three feet wider than the *Nymphe* – much larger.

Poor dear Pearse is numbered with the slain – Plane and Norway slightly wounded – old Nicholls safe. God be praised for his mercy to myself, and Israel, and all of us!

                                                   Yours ever, E. P.

Be kind to Susan. Go over and comfort her; I cannot write to poor Pearse's mother for my life – do send her a note: I really cannot. I loved him, poor fellow, and he deserved it. *June 20, 1793.*

The magnanimous manners that existed between the commanders of the two sides (we have already heard each side conversing and cheering before the action) is exemplified by correspondence *after* the battle. Indeed, this mutual respect between the combatants was apparent in both world wars and no doubt it is alive today. The services of each side dissociate themselves from the dangerous puffing and blowing of the politicians, but they salute one another.

Turn then to Appendix 'D' and read the reply, to a letter of sympathy by Captain Pellew to the widow, of his recent adversary, Captain Millon of the *Cleopatre*.

Edward Ostler, from whose work I draw freely and gratefully for this, my short memoir, writing in 1834 and still close to the events chronicled above, informs us that

> The capture of the first frigate in a war is always an object of much interest; and the circumstances of the late action, the merit of which was enhanced by the skill and gallantry of the enemy, gave additional importance to Captain Pellew's success. 'I never doubted,' Lord Howe (Admiral of the Fleet) told him, 'that you would take a French frigate; but the manner in which you have done it will establish an example set for the war'.

Official recognition was soon to come. Captain Pellew, the hero from Cornwall, was introduced to the King on 29th June 1793, receiving the honour of knighthood. The King presented him to the Queen with the rather cryptic remark, 'This is *our* friend.'

Sir Edward, as we can now proudly call this Cornish hero, was appointed to another frigate. I might mention that frigates were the dashing arm of the Navy then, in the same way that destroyers were in the twentieth century, glamour being consequently bestowed by them on their crews.

The *Arethusa*, to which he was appointed as captain, was a forty-four gun frigate with eighteen pounders on the main-deck, and thirty-two pounders on the quarter-deck and foc'sle. Let me interpolate that the weights refer to the cannon ball fired.

Small squadrons of the enemy ships at this time were creating damage to our shipping in the mouth of the Channel. To
counter this, Sir Edward convinced his senior officers and the
Admiralty that the thing to do was to break with naval
practice and to limit the number of frigates attached to the
fleet and form them into an independent cruising squadron,
based at Falmouth.

The force was placed under the command of Commodore
Sir John Borlase Warren, becoming known as the Western
Squadrons. Their successes came so soon, and were so frequent that their reputation for dashing enterprise made it the
most sought after command to be in.

The thrill of his appointment to this command surely
satisfied Sir Edward's inclinations as a sea-going captain, the
alertness required and the tenseness of cruising in enemy
waters, the hovering necessary, close in to the enemy's coast,
or sweeping the seas well off it, the chase by a single ship
detached to observe a suspicious stranger, or by the whole
squadron, full sail to overtake an enemy group, and its consequence, an action.

In a big line-of-battle ship, with its high discipline, there
was less demand for individual enterprise, no opportunity for
exploits where all depended on rapidity and daring.

In the middle of April 1794, Commodore Warren and his
frigates had their first engagement with the enemy off the
Brittany coast. Suffice it to say here that the enemy ships were
forced to surrender after a fierce action, *Arethusa* earning her
share of praise, epitomised in this note from the Commodore
transferred to Sir Edward at sea as the enemy struck:

My dear Pellew,
    I shall ever hold myself indebted, and under infinite
obligations to you, for the noble and gallant support you
gave me today.
    God bless you and all yours
                                Yours etc.
                                J.B. Warren.

I hope my readers agree with my emphasis on providing opportunity for reading letters, written by participants or witnesses, of historic or dramatic portent. They bring with them the same sense of immediacy that they provided for the recipient of the time in fact. The years between vanish, and in one step backwards a realm is reached in which time has no place in one's emotions, for they may be aroused by words on paper, the same words that inspired the writer a hundred, two hundred years ago, though I do not pretend that the difference in custom and morals does not vary their meaning.

Well, that being said, let me provide you with another letter to enable us to share in the pride of our distinguished Cornish sea captain. This time the letter is from none other than the great Earl of Chatham, First Lord of the Admiralty:

Dear Sir,
    I have but a moment to answer your letter, which I have received this morning, with infinite pleasure; and to say that I am extremely happy the same success and honour attend you in the *Arethusa* as in the *Nymphe*. I shall be very glad to see you while you are refitting, as soon as your leg will permit it, and which, I am happy to hear, is only a sprain,
                         Your very faithful, humble servant,
                         Chatham.

Action came plentifully during the next twelve months while Sir Edward was with the Western Squadron in the *Arethusa*.

In April 1794, in an action off the Île de Bas he captured the *Pomone* and brought her into Portsmouth. She was a bigger frigate than the *Arethusa*. Three months later another French squadron was encountered and, in a brilliant tactical manoeuvre by Sir Edward, was driven ashore.

It was October before the French were encountered again, this time close to the Cornish coast. It was the morning of 20th April when the squadron was lying-to off the Lizard. A large ship was seen coming in from seaward; then it tacked and stood off without acknowledging the signal of the day.

There was a stiff breeze off the land and the British ships gave chase, led by the *Indefatigable*, in which was Sir Edward in command. Fifteen hours later, the French ship, the *Virginie*, was still ahead but came within range at last, and with almost the first shot scored a hit which killed seven of the enemy at one of the quarter-deck guns. The *Indefatigable* was struck at her mainmast when Sir Edward had a very narrow escape. The main-top-mast was shot away, disabling the mainyard when a tangled mass of rigging and wood came tumbling around him.

Both ships were in a bad state. The action had taken an hour and a half, and by now several frigates had arrived on the scene and the *Virginie* surrendered.

A boat was sent to her from the *Indefatigable* to fetch the gallant French captain, Jacques Bergeret, who was very emotional, and weeping bitterly. He enquired by whom had he been captured? When told it was Pellew, he allegedly exclaimed, 'Oh, that is the most fortunate man that ever lived! He takes everything, and now he takes the finest frigate in France!'

Let us change the subject now, and turn away from Sir Edward's exploits as a commander at sea against the enemy, and be witness of an event in which he distinguished himself in harbour one evening in January 1796.

If you stand on Plymouth Hoe at the Citadel end and look down at the Sound below, you will see across the fairly narrow entrance to Catwater the promontory (for want of a better description) of Mount Batten which forms the other side to the entrance to this pool of sheltered water, as compared to that of Plymouth Sound.

The *Indefatigable* was lying in Hamoaze on the western side opposite Mount Batten. Her captain, Sir Edward, was in a carriage going to a private dinner ashore; there was a gale blowing, but *Indefatigable* he knew well was lying snug and secure so that he felt free to enjoy his outing. However, on his way he was confronted by crowds running to the Hoe, and having ascertained the cause, he jumped from his carriage and joined them, having been told that a large East Indiaman, the *Dutton*, had broken loose from her mooring in the Sound and had drifted swiftly ashore under the Citadel. This was not quite correct in detail, but no matter.

The *Dutton*, it appeared, was employed as a transport vessel by the Government and had on board men of the Queen's regiment. She had been driven by the weather into Plymouth while at the outset of her voyage to the East Indies.

It was the 'outset' only in terms of the mileage she had covered, for the weather in the Channel had so continuously been against her as she tried to make her way down Channel against contrary winds that seven weeks had been taken up before she made Plymouth.

The *Dutton* was intending to re-fill her water casks when, due to the gale having shifted a vital navigational buoy off Mount Batten, she touched ground and lost her rudder before reaching the Catwater. Now unmanageable, she fell off and grounded under the Citadel, rolling heavily, her broadside to the waves.

While we imagine Pellew hastily leaving the dinner table and rushing down through the tumult of the stormy January afternoon to see what he could do, let us for a moment consider those onboard the *Dutton*, now stranded and buffeted by wind and tempest, impaled on the seabed, perhaps only fifty yards from the shore.

We know what they must be feeling onboard; anxious, cold and scared, but hopeful, for at least, they could reasonably expect, they were lucky to be aground so near the shore, just a stone's throw away.

But were they right in finding comfort in this? Curiously enough, just a few miles to the westward, in Mount's Bay, Henry Trengrouse, the cabinet maker, whom we met, briefly, in connection with Humphry Davy, would have known otherwise because for some years he had been experimenting with a device to save lives on just such an occasion as this. I refer to his rocket apparatus which, when fired, would shoot above the raging surf between ship and shore dragging as its tail a line to be caught by the crew. They were to haul in on this line which, in turn, would haul in a rope to which a cradle was suspended. This cradle was to be hauled to and fro with a crew member in it until all had been taken off *above* the sea.

In devising this apparatus, Trengrouse had gone to great lengths to analyse, precisely, the forces in terms of undertow and wind and waves that were involved when a ship was blown ashore.

So let Trengrouse himself tell us what the problems were in a wreck such as the *Dutton*. It's quite something: I take it from his book *Shipwreck Investigated, Ch. IX*, published a few years later in 1817:

I believe what follows to be a fair Delineation of Shipwreck in one of its milder forms. After buffeting with the waves the sailors on board are now within sixty, perhaps within forty, yards of the shore where numbers of people are assembled, waiting, ready, eager to afford all possible assistance – and who would willingly go to the wreck, and bring on their backs to the shore, the poor weatherbeaten sailors; but, alas, they are outside their reach.

It is true the distance is small that parts them, but even that small space is occupied by a tremendous enemy, – an angry surf which awes them to keep a respectful distance as tho' it were jealous lest the poor shivering fellows upon the wreck should be rescued from becoming its victims.

They now view their situation with horror, for they see no way to *insure* their deliverance; they have not any *means* to accomplish it! they had flattered themselves much from the appearance of the shore – well – it has not altered – it is the same, and yet invites them to tread its surface, but, alas, they are restrained by the impassable gulph that interposes. Though their vessel is on the ground, they are afloat on the waves of doubt and uncertainty, which are big with horror and dismay, for notwithstanding their case among ship-wrecks is not of the worst sort, yet it is bad; it is dreadful enough to shake their confidence and to alarm their fears.

They now find themselves exposed to danger, not of the common kind; danger far surpassing in terrors what they had anticipated; for they were before strangers to ship-wreck; only a few onboard had experienced it, and very many had never beheld it with their eyes. In the midst of heavy storms they had been accustomed to *float upon* the 'white-top wave', but *now* they are frequently enveloped in its enraged bosom and covered with its indignant foam. Their favourite vessel already creaks and cries, and threatens to recede from their close embraces by separating from beneath them ... yet she forbears.

The retiring tide favours keeping her together for a little longer – but the poor disconcerted sailors do not heed this friendly circumstance, their minds are already unhinged – they are confused in their ideas – distressed in their situation – each one shifts for himself. The *good swimmer* trusts to his *skills* – the *ordinary* one marks the *shortness* of the *distance*. The shore is viewed with anxiety by all – the desperate attempt is undertaken – they plunge into the sea – they swim – but alas! – the ebb tide which favoured their pre-servation while upon the wreck, now promotes their destruction! They find it hard work to make any progress toward the shore – they exert all their strength and skill – they tug hard – but, alas! the breakers, too, are united against them, and in succession, with furious dash, beat them to the bottom – they struggle – most of them struggle their last, and perish! a few only reach the land.

All through his life Sir Edward showed a genius for leadership, and the courage that it demanded: and the situa-tion he beheld of the chaos onboard the storm-battered *Dutton* as he viewed it from the surf-whipped shore-line at the foot of the Citadel, could have left him in no doubt that his resources would have to be stretched to the absolute limit to bring order to the ship and crew.

Arrived at the scene of this dramatic disaster, Pellew

quickly assessed the situation and found it was evident that
the loss of nearly all on board, some six hundred people, was
inevitable unless the terrified victims could be reassured by a
leader who could take charge. The ship, it appeared, was
without the appropriate officers, who somehow had escaped
ashore. Confronting these officers, to a background of
thunderous noise from wind and crashing seas and slinging
spray, and shouts and screams from those clinging to the
sloping deck till a wave of furious water dislodged a precious
hold, to this background Sir Edward exhorted them to return
onboard, hazardous though that was; but they refused. He
tried another source from among the spectators, namely, port
pilots and others to whom he offered rewards. Getting no
support, he exclaimed, 'Then I'll go myself.'

The danger of reaching the drowning ship through the surf
and rip-tide was made worse by the ship's masts having
crashed down, bringing with them a tangle of rigging and
spars and violently flapping canvas; and always the caco-
phony of noise.

He did, in fact, receive an injury to his back as he fought his
way through the maelstrom to the ship, and this was reflected
when all was over by his having to go to bed and stay in bed
for more than a week.

Let us imagine, now, that we were one of the passengers in
this despairing situation onboard, and how wonderful was the
change in our situation when this calm, authoritative man
appeared from nowhere and addressed us.

Shouting through the storm's roar he assured us that everyone would be saved provided we did exactly what he said, if
they quietly obeyed his orders, that he would be the last to
quit the wreck; but that he would run anyone through with his
sword if he disobeyed.

Sir Edward was already a well-known name, and this
helped him to gain immediate authority over the despairing
community. The calmness and strength of character he
displayed inspired this confidence, too. His words were
received with three hearty cheers which pierced the discord of

the storm to be echoed by those hearing them on shore.

The officers of *Indefatigable*, though not knowing their captain was now onboard the *Dutton*, were doing all in their power to bring assistance. Her barge and her launch were brought to the harrowing scene but found it quite impossible to come alongside the wreck.

A small boat from a merchant vessel was more successful, courageously helped by Mr Edsell, signal midshipman to the Port Admiral, and by Mr Coghlan, mate of this vessel, who, at the risk of their lives, helped it alongside. The waves, smashing down on to the hull and tossing the small boat violently about as the men held it alongside, at the same time preventing it crashing, all but proved too much for their efforts.

However, the ends of two hawsers were got ashore and Sir Edward contrived two cradles (e.g. the basis of Trengrouse's experiments in Mount's Bay), to be slung upon them with travelling ropes to pass backwards and forwards between the ship and the beach.

Each hawser was held on shore by a number of men who watched the rolling of the wreck, and its heavy bumping on the bottom, and kept the ropes tight and steady. The hull was being brutally treated by the incoming surf, lifting and dropping it onto the seabed as freely as though it were a plaything; and it was realised it was only a question of time before it split and broke up, spilling those onboard into the turbulent undertow.

At length a cutter arrived from the dockyard which was able to approach and, the tide being by now at half-ebb, a few passengers were able to be taken aboard it.

Sir Edward directed operations, with his sword drawn, a stance with serious undertones for, apart from it being good for the morale seeing him standing confidently with his sword at the ready, he was anxious about drunken soldiers who had got at the spirits store before he came aboard and were now drunk and unpredictable.

As the women and children were helped into the cutter Sir

Edward was able to comfort one of the mothers with a child only three weeks old when she had to be separated from it in order to facilitate the rescue. Her reaction of confidence in him when he promised that the infant would be safe in his care, gave him more pleasure than the success of his attempt to save it. In all, some five hundred people were saved.

Sir Edward, spectacular as his career was, himself was a modest man; and perhaps this could not be more deftly displayed than in the phrasing of the entry in the *Indefatigable's* logbook. It consisted of one short sentence: 'Sent two boats to the assistance of a ship on shore in the Sound,' and that is all.

He had, of course, officially to inform the Commander-in-Chief, Plymouth, Vice-Admiral Onslow, of the event notwithstanding it was witnessed by thousands of people watching the drama. Edward, as one might expect, found this embarrassingly immodest, and he made virtually no mention of himself at all:

> Dear Sir,
> I hope it happened to me this afternoon to be serviceable to the unhappy sufferers on board the *Dutton*: and I have much satisfaction in saying that every soul in her was taken out before I left her, except the first mate, boatswain and third mate, who attended the hauling ropes to the shore, and they eased me on shore by the hawser.
> It is not possible to refrain from speaking raptures of the handsome conduct of Mr Hemmings, the master-attendant, who, at the imminent risk to his life, saved hundreds. If I had not hurt my leg, and been otherwise much bruised, I would have waited on you [reported personally]: but hope this will be passable excuse.
> I am, with respect ...... etc., etc.

Edward's modesty was unable to stem the clamour of praise that now assailed him. The Corporation of Plymouth voted him the Freedom of the town and the merchants of Liverpool (the *Dutton*'s home-port) presented him with a fine service of plate; and on 5th March he was created a baronet as Sir Edward Pellew, of Treverry.

However, it was not long before Sir Edward and his frigates were out on active patrol again and in action. On 9th March, the *Indefatigable* sailed from Falmouth with the *Revolutionaire* (a captured frigate) *Argo*, *Amazon* and *Concorde* (another captured vessel), looking a splendid sight as, leaving with the wind they sped, one after the other, past Black Rock, still there today, that visual link for us with our seamen centuries back.

And now, please, a word to you, my reader. Sensitive to the fact that an author can easily lose your interest if he overdoes his own enthusiasm, I am going to pause here in my study of this brilliant, brave and elegant Cornishman, and deflect you from having to follow the sequence of his life story, with me as your guide, any longer.

I have, I hope, by now introduced you to his virtues and his style, in a manner that will have whetted your interest, and, indeed, stirred your pride. Sir Edward Pellew's career continued in spectacular fashion, and further study of it in detail can be obtained from Ostler's *Life*, published in 1835. But now I am going to refresh you with his influence on England's fortunes from another viewpoint, his own viewpoint, his official report to the Admiralty of a unique operation played out in enemy waters nearly a thousand miles from home. It is a most unusual action which he describes in his own words; so, confident in the approval of his benificent shade, I present it herewith. But first, I must set the scene, and this I can dispose of in a few words.

Owing to recent political events (1816), there were a large number of Christian slaves held by the Dey of Algiers, and it was deemed very necessary to free them. For this purpose an operation was mounted from England under the command of Pellew who, consequent on his record of successes was by now elevated to the peerage. To our Cornish chagrin he chose the title that links him to Devon, namely, Lord Exmouth of Canonteign, which was the name of an estate he had purchased. How much sweeter to Cornish ears it would be if this great sailor and patriot had still possessed the estate of Trefusis on the shores of Falmouth Harbour which had also been his. And now for his Despatch to the Admiralty; it is full of detail of interest to both sailor and layman.

'*Queen Charlotte*, Algiers Bay, 28 August 1816 ... My thanks are justly due for the honour and confidence his Majesty's Ministers have been pleased to repose on my zeal on this highly important occasion ... Would to God that in the attainment of this object I had not deeply to lament the severe loss of so many gallant officers and men.

'The battle was fairly at issue between a handful of Britons, in the noble cause of Christianity, and a horde of Fanatics assembled round their city, and enclosed within its fortifications, to obey the dictates of their Despot.

'The cause of God and humanity prevailed; and so devoted was every creature in the Fleet that even British women served at the guns with their husbands, and during a contest of many hours, never shrank from danger but animated all around them.

'If ever it can be permitted for an officer to depart from the usual forms of naval correspondence on any occasion, I trust I shall find, in the indulgence of my superiors, and of my Country, excuses for having thus to intrude my own sentiments; and I confine myself to their liberality.

'Their Lordships will have already been informed by the sloop *Jasper* of my proceedings up to the 14 inst, on which day I broke ground from Gibraltar after a vexatious detention of four days by a foul wind. The fleet, complete in all its points, with the addition of five gunboats fitted at Gibraltar, departed in the highest spirits and expecting to reach their destination in three days, but an adverse wind destroyed the expectation of an early arrival which was serious in consequence of my hearing the day I sailed from Gibraltar, that a large army had been assembled and that very considerable defence works were being thrown up, not only on both flanks of the city but also immediately about the entrance to the Mole.

'From this I feared that my intention of making that point my principal object of attack had been discovered by the Dey by the same means that he had heard of the Expedition.

'This intelligence was on the following night greatly confirmed by the *Prometheus* which I had despatched to Algiers some time before to endeavour to get the Consul away. Captain Dashwood had with difficulty succeeded in bringing away, disguised in midshipman's uniform, his wife and daughter, leaving a boat to bring off their infant child, coming down in a basket with the surgeon who thought he had calmed it; but it unhappily cried in the gateway, and, in consequence, the surgeon, three midshipmen and in all, eighteen persons, were seized and confined as slaves in the usual dungeons. The child was sent off next morning by the Dey, and, as a solitary instance of his humanity, it ought to be recorded by me.

'Captain Dashwood further confirmed that about 40,000 men had been brought down from the interior and that they were indefatigably employed on the batteries, gunboats, etc., and everywhere strengthening their defences.

'All the Dey's ships were in port, and between forty and fifty gun and mortar boats ready, with several more in forward repair. The Dey had closely confined the Consul and refused either to give him up, or to promise his personal safety.

'From the continuance of adverse winds and calms [our fleet] did not make sight of the city of Algiers until the 26th, and next morning, at daybreak it was still not so near as I intended.

'As the ships were becalmed, I embraced this opportunity of despatching a boat with a flag of truce directing the officer to wait two or three hours for the Dey's answer, at which time, if no reply was sent he was to return to the flag-ship.

'He was met near the Mole by the captain of the port, who, on being told that the answer was expected in one hour, replied that it was impossible.

'The fleet at this time, by the springing up of a breeze, had reached the Bay, and were preparing the flotilla and boats for service, until near two o'clock when, observing my officer returning with the signal flying that no answer had been received, I instantly made the signal to know if ships were all ready; which, being answered in the affirmative, the *Queen Charlotte* bore up, followed by the fleet, for their appointed stations. The flat [ship] leading in the prescribed order, was anchored at the entrance of the Mole, at about fifty yards distance [I must just interpolate here to ask you to imagine the electric tension in the air, in each and every ship as all waited for the vacuum to collapse, for the guns to fire their roaring cannonades in a ferment of blood and destruction].

'But still not a gun had been fired and I began to suspect a full compliance with the terms which had been so many hours in their hands.

'At this period of profound silence, a shot was fired at us from the Mole, and two of the ships from the northward then following. This was promptly returned by the *Queen Charlotte*, and thus commenced a fire as animated and well supported as I believe was ever witnessed, from a quarter before three until nine in the evening, without intermission, and which did not cease altogether till half-past eleven.

'To look farther along the line than immediately around me was perfectly impossible; but so well-grounded was my confidence in the gallant officers I had the honour to command, that my mind was left perfectly free to attend to other objects; and I knew them in their stations only by the destructive effect of their fire upon the walls and batteries to which they were opposed.

'After sunset I received a message from Rear-Admiral Milne conveying to me the severe loss the *Impregnable* was sustaining, having then one hundred and fifty killed and wounded, and requesting I would, if possible, send him a frigate to divert some of the fire he was under.

'The *Glasgow* near me, immediately weighed, but the wind had been driven away by the cannonade and she was obliged to anchor again, having obtained a rather better position than before.

'I had at this time sent orders to the *explosion vessel* to bring her into the Mole, but the Rear-Admiral having thought she might do him essential service if exploded under the battery in his front, I desired Captain Powell to carry my orders to this vessel to that effect, where he staid until it was executed.

'I desired also the Rear-Admiral might be informed that many of the enemy ships being now in flames, and the destruction of the whole certain, I considered I had executed the most important part of my instructions, and should make every preparation for withdrawing my ships, and desired he would do so with his division.

'There were awful moments during this conflict which I cannot attempt to describe, occasioned by firing the fire-ships so close to us. I had long resisted the eager entreaties of several around me to make the attempt on the outer frigate distant about a hundred yards which, at length, I gave in to: and Major Gosett at my side, who had been eager to land his corps of Cornish miners, pressed most anxiously for permission to accompany Lieutenant Richards in the ship's barge. The frigate was instantly boarded and in ten minutes was in a perfect blaze. A gallant young midshipman in rocket boat No 8, although forbidden, was led by his ardent spirit to follow in support of the barge; in which attempt he was desperately wounded, his brother officer killed and nine of his crew.

'The enemy's batteries around my division were about ten o'clock silenced and in a state of perfect ruin and dilapidation; and the fire of this ship [*Queen Charlotte*] was reserved as much as possible to save powder and to reply to a few guns now and again bearing upon us; although a fort on the upper angle of the city, on which our guns could not be brought to bear, continued to annoy the ships by shot and shells, during the whole time.

'Providence at this interval gave to my anxious wishes the usual land-wind common to this bay. We were all hands warping and towing off, and by the help of the light air, the whole fleet were under sail, and came to anchor out of reach of shot and shells about two in the morning, after twelve hours incessant labour.

'The flotilla of mortar, gun, and rocket-boats, under the direction of their various artillery officers shared in the honours of the day and performed good service. It was by their fire that all the ships in the port, with the exception of the outer frigate *were in flames*, which extended rapidly over the whole arsenal, storehouses, and gun-boats exhibiting a spectacle of awful grandeur and interest no pen can describe.

'The shells and the bombs were admirably well thrown by the Royal Marine Artillery; and although thrown directly across and over us, not an accident I know of ever occurred in any ship.

'The whole was conducted in perfect silence, and such a thing as a cheer I never heard in any part of the line ... the action will be remembered by these barbarians for ever.'

Edward Pellew of Penzance, by now Lord Exmouth of Canonteign, concluded his report with citations in favour of many of the officers and men who were engaged in the successful operation.

In this short memoir of a most distinguished Cornishman, we have, I believe, touched on enough aspects of his career to form a judgement of the *man*; but much I have left untold, partly because, to laymen, one battle at sea is much like another in principle; and so, rather than risk turning the reader away under a veil of ennui, I am going to take leave of the gallant admiral, and call on him just once more, but this time in his retirement, when he is nearer seventy than sixty, and showing him trying to oblige an old friend with a favour of a kind that reads today as though it were yesterday.

Edward had this boyhood friend, a fellow Cornishman whom I also feel to be a friend though a century and a half has passed since the time I speak of. Richard Polwhele was a clergyman and an historian, and his seven volumes of *The History of Cornwall* are the bridge that guides one to his friendship. He may be remote in time for me, but at the period of the correspondence to which I am about to refer, he was vicar of the church at Newlyn East, a village but three miles from where I live.

Here follows, then, correspondence from a father to his friend, seeking the best for his young son, a not unfamiliar instinct for a parent today.

I draw this correspondence from Polwhele's *Reminiscences*, vol. 1, published in 1836. Polwhele has written a letter to Exmouth to which the retired Admiral replies:

London, 21 July 1821

My dear Sir,

Nothing but the hurry and bustle of the Coronation should have prevented me answering your letter. I am very sorry your son should have been so unfortunate, and I regret it the more my total inability to help him. I have been exerting myself to get a young friend afloat ever since I struck my flag, without effect; and I fear you will find it extremely hard unless you should have any friend commissioned to a new ship.

The former patronage of captains is now nearly all swallowed up by the unsatiated Admiralty, who are never contented.

Believe me, my dear Sir, most faithfully yours,

Exmouth.

Three years later, the request was brought up again, and Exmouth replied:

31 Dec. 1824

My dear Sir,

I have received your friendly note, and I hope I need scarcely profess my inclination to render you services in the way you have pointed out, if it had been in my power, but the fact is quite the contrary; and I have been above a year using all my exertions to place the eleventh child of a friend and neighbour without success.

The only chance of getting a boy on a ship's books must now be done through your acquaintance with any Captain about to be commissioned to a ship, and this only happens when the Stations are relieving, every three years.

But your effectual way will be through Lord Melville to send your son out to some flag officer in command, on his list of promotion; there is no other way nowadays; the whole patronage of the Navy of the Country is vested in one man, and a great evil to the Country it is. An Admiral on half-pay after 50 years service, has no more interest than your parish clerk; and unless called for by a war, may as well ask for a bishopric as promotion for a young friend during this piping peace.

I am very glad to hear you are in good health, and so I hope are all your family.

Ever your sincere old friend,

Exmouth.

VI

Unsettling Interlude

It is not often that I feel any emotion other than contentment while with *Spray* sailing on our friendly enemy, the sea. Even in conditions of rough and rain-dowsed weather, with fading light and the night ahead of us I may feel somewhat tense, but not unsettled.

But now, the spectre of fire invades my consciousness, the picture we have just seen of Lord Exmouth's bombardment of Algiers, leaving when, as he said, 'All the enemy ships in port were on fire, thanks to our fireships and rocket guns, and flames enveloped the whole arsenal, the storehouses and gunboats exhibiting a spectacle of *awful grandeur*...'

It is this picture that disturbs me, for *Spray* is now sailing very near the track that the victorious fleet would have passed over as they made for Falmouth to discharge the most urgent cases among their casualties. On board were a total of more than twelve hundred ill or wounded.

It is true that fire was the means that brought the operation success; but fire is also the most terrifying intruder in a ship imaginable, the unspoken anxiety of all onboard, as it is all-consuming; but in the ghost fleet of Lord Exmouth in whose wake we are now sailing, though destruction by fire was spared them, there is no doubt that among the wounded are likely to be a number who suffered burns from accidents such as with powder at the guns. Survivors of such wounds and others had to endure the limitations of the surgeon's facilities.

A naval surgeon's difficulties are stated by Edward Ives in his *Voyage from England to India* (1773):

At the very instant when I was amputating the limb of one of our wounded seamen I met with an almost continual interruption from the rest of his companions who were in the like circumstances; some pouring forth the most piercing cries to be taken care of, while others seized my arms in their earnestness of being relieved, even at the time when I was passing the needle for securing the divided blood vessels by a ligature. Surely at the time when such operations were in contemplation, the operator's mind as well as body ought to be as little agitated as possible, and the very shaking of the lower gundeck, owing to the recoil of the large cannon which are placed just above his head, is of itself sufficient to incommode a surgeon ...

to say nothing of the movement of the ship!

In his *Burns of Sea Battles*, published by the National Maritime Museum Surgeon Vice-Admiral James Watt tells of an horrific situation a young surgeon found himself in; the Journal of the *Theseus* for the year 1799 records that a midshipman and a carpenter were defusing some shells on deck with an auger, mallet and spike. This caused a violent explosion and the young surgeon was saddled with eighty-seven casualties.

Then, a few days later, Napoleon retreated from Acre and the British ships captured several French vessels whose seamen were suffering from the plague which rapidly spread to the British ships. The poor surgeon, Robert Tainsh, then had the eighty-seven casualties from the explosion, and a rapidly spreading infection of the plague to try and cope with, too.

I have already spoken of the latent apprehension of fire in the minds of seamen; but fortunately that fear is seldom realised. However, it is, sometimes, and by me, for example.

Normally, I would not consider my short chronicle of the occasion worth recording here in this postscript to my memoir of Lord Exmouth. However, I do so, but only for the rather extraordinary coincidental twist that ties it up at the end.

I shall copy out what I wrote in my journal as a Naval Cadet going out to the Mediterranean to join his first ship at Malta, after leaving the Royal Naval College, over fifty years ago. The ship was an old four-funnelled, coal-burning cruiser, HMS *Dartmouth*:

'Our arrival at Gibraltar coincided with our first day in white uniform, so everyone looked scrupulously clean and cool. One can have no idea what it feels like to be familiar with living among men in dark blue, and then, all at once, they come down one morning to breakfast in soft, scrupulous white.

'Our scrupulous whiteness, however, was not to last long, because, as soon as we had berthed at nine o'clock we started coaling ship, and the whole ship's company, the officers and the Padre as well, toiled through that hot September day, and sweated shovelling tons and tons of coal into baskets, endless baskets, carrying them up the gang-plank to the ship and tipping the coal down into the bunkers.

'Coal dust was everywhere, and with it, acute discomfort, but I revelled in every minute of it. Every so often a tub of lime juice was sent round, and what bliss it was to drink and drink the soothing liquid and wash away the foul dust that choked us!

'After every hour, a signal was hoisted at the masthead denoting the number of tons taken in during that hour, and a cheer would go up as each record was smashed. I was proud to belong to a body of men who applied themselves so ceaselessly at work, the reward for which only bore them further and further away from home.

'On the second day out from Gibraltar on our way to Malta, an interesting experience befell us. I was on duty on the bridge as cadet of the watch, with the captain and navigator. Suddenly, a seaman hurried up to the bridge from below decks.

'He saluted the captain and reported that No 1 stokehold fire had spread to the coal bunker itself, and was out of hand. And the new paint on the boiler itself, with a lot of coal dust in the boiler room, had caught fire and was burning fiercely.

'Fire parties were hastily summoned, and very soon hoses were playing through the hatch on the flames below.

'By now, the ship was standing-to with no way on her, and everyone onboard unfamiliar with the routine for dealing with such an emergency: for the *Dartmouth* was being used as a trooping ship, being manned by men who would be relieving others on the China Station. The latter would man the ship taking them home.

'The black smoke was now pouring out of the hatch so that to stifle the air the captain's duty was to order it to be closed, not knowing if a stoker or more was trapped in it down there.

'I began to feel somewhat alarmed, for I could see that men were unable to walk on deck because of it becoming nearly red hot, until a hose played on it. This quelled it in showers of white billows of steam glistening in the sun, from which we on the bridge were protected from its direct rays by a taut canvas awning stretched from side to side.

'Suddenly, a midshipman from the engineer officer appeared and announced that it had just been discovered that the compartment next to the stokehold and forward of it was the torpedo warhead magazine and should they flood it? He added as almost an afterthought that this bulkhead was red hot!

'This was the first time I had ever been faced with a serious emergency and it did not take more than an instant for it to cause an instinctive reaction to the immediate prospect of being blown sky high. That reaction would hardly have been efficacious for it took the form of me darting to the side of the bridge, and leaning out from under the awning so at least I would not hit my head as we blew up, but have a clear run skywards. Well, well.'

And now for the twist of coincidence. Later, when things had calmed down and we knew the ship was not going to blow up, I was ordered to make the navigator a cup of ship's chocolate, a lovely, rich and wholesome beverage, unlikely to be the same today. He was seated at the chart with his back to me when I brought him the cup.

Reaching over his shoulder I placed the cup just above the heading of the chart which was titled 'Bay of Algiers' – a name of not much consequence to me then, but of potent meaning to me today.

VII

Opie, John, painter

It is now close on midnight on this moonless night of early summer, and *Spray* and I are sailing just for the fun of it. The ghost fleet of Lord Exmouth returning home we have allowed to quit our ken, leaving us to merge with the night and the past off Falmouth Bay.

The black velvet sky has a canopy of stars, their light mirrored like the dust of diamonds on the ruffled black waters beneath. And *Spray* is alone in the silent night except for the sound of unhurried contentment of lapping water against her pinewood hull, the splash of wavelet on the bow as the gentle breeze eases us along at $2\frac{1}{2}$ knots.

There is no place where one is closer to nature, nor more exposed to her humours, than in an engineless boat at sea, at night, alone.

Apart from the starlight and the dying dollops of saffron lights of Falmouth at the end of this day, there is only the pale red glow of my port navigation light, seen momentarily now and then, when *Spray's* gentle prancing permits it, on the lovely curved surface of the jib. When I change course, the friendly red glow vanishes as we go about and in its place is the cold blue green of the starboard light.

We are not entirely left to our own resources, for the lighthouse on St Anthony's Point is flashing its beam at us as though to say we understand each other, I'm here for you, use me.

These bonds between seafarers, and for them, are unseen and uncalled for in port, but once out in the open sea the link between ships and their crews, with other ships and crews, are very evident and never fail to stir the heart whenever visual contact is made, be it ocean liner with *Spray*, or with giant tanker. A sighting provokes alertness, curiosity, and a marshalling of skills and navigational resources, because the bond of which I speak is forged by mutual awareness and experience of the sudden dangers that can appear at sea. These are fed by complex combinations of wind and currents and compasses, humidity and temperature and poor look-out.

With training behind one in the arts of navigation with sextant, chart and compass, and in the craft of seamanship with storm and sail and screw, with tides and currents and shallows and channels and streams, with these ingredients and the many others that go to the making of a seaman, the joy of the élite is yours at sea.

And it does not only relate to those vessels you see on the horizon today, but for centuries the camaraderie, or the respect by enemy of one for the other, have been present here on this black sea, refreshed by the clear, Cornish waters of the Fal and Helford rivers. Fleets, great arrays of ships, have come and gone. Through these waters, visually identical to what *Spray* and I delight in now, hulls have passed barnacled from long voyages, or freshly cleaned and careened for the next sea adventure.

Great arrays of ships, whole fleets have passed here, and little ones with big hearts; furtive ones on unlawful occasions dodging the lights of the Revenue boat; and now *Spray*, with me aboard, enraptured by the canopy of stars reflected on the restless sea, and the loom of the Eddystone to the east, the Lizard light to the west, and St Anthony light just over there two or three cables from Black Rock.

I come to realise that the scenes I envisage on this peaceful night do not relate to their true content which almost invariably involves stress or strain; but time softens the hue of the reality of the past, and the romantic aura it has for me is not disturbed. I indulge myself in it, in my good fortune in living this moment, which I am going to prolong by heaving-to and getting myself a cup of coffee. I pull in on the weather fore-sheet, make it fast, then ease out the main and make that fast; and now I enjoy the compliment that *Spray* pays me by looking after herself on this beautiful night, on this beautiful sea. I am reminded of my good fortune in possessing a paint- ing of a night scene at sea, surely an appallingly difficult subject for an artist to realise successfully. The picture I have is one I found in the antique shop at Leedstown many years ago. It is a picture of the Wolf Rock lighthouse as seen from a passing boat on a half-moonlit night with a tumbling sea, and is a triumph for the unknown artist. I have so often wondered to whom I should be grateful for its never failing gift of recall- ing such a magic scene for me.

Recalling this picture now, with the lights of three other lighthouses in view, I fall to wonder why Cornwall has not provided artists of note to supplement the long list of its famous sons in other spheres of activity. History pinpoints none of note – none except one – and not even one who captured for us the Cornish scene until there arrived the talent of the Newlyn and St Ives painters at the beginning of our own century.

However, you may have noted I have suggested there is an exception: there is, indeed; Opie, John Opie, but even he has left with us little of the Cornish scene at the turn of the eighteenth century in which he lived, his having preferred the London fashionable scene. [Appendix E]

He died an honoured Associate of the Royal Academy, and I can indicate in no better way the stature in society of this St Agnes parishioner, son of the village carpenter, than com- mencing our study with the end for the beginning.

He was buried in St Paul's Cathedral, as was Sir Joshua Reynolds of the same period, on 20th April 1807; and there follows, herewith, a description of the funeral pageant. I draw from Ada Earland's *John Opie and his Circle*, published by Hutchinson in 1911.

In part, I relate the following account of mine for its fascina- tion to many people of today who have no idea of the importance attached to mourning by a society that for centuries had revelled in it: and rules and strictures on behaviour were prevalent to an awesome degree even in my lifetime.

But when John Opie died the people involved were fêted to what can only be described as a mournful pageant, while the relatives enjoyed weeks of uncomfortable confinement.

Opie died on 9th April, and between then and the 20th, the day of the funeral, the widow had to remain in a darkened house. Surrounding her were all the artefacts of woe that a barbarous custom could suggest to keep her lowered vitality low. Even the door-knocker was muffled in flannel and straw was laid on the road outside. Visitors, who thought of themselves as appropriately equipped for mourning, were assessed as welcome according to the degree of dejection in their faces and manner.

John Opie, the central figure of this occasion, now at rest from his labours, held state in a room hung with black materials and lit with candles of yellow wax placed in sconces round the walls.

His old friend, John Penwarne, assumed charge of the funeral arrangement, and all cards of invitation were sent out in his name, bidding guests to assemble at the house at eleven o'clock.

On the day of the funeral, mutes [professional, dumb funeral attendants] took up their posts at the front door, and stood there in attitudes of dejection. The mourners, on arrival, were regaled with wine and cake. At one o'clock the procession started off.

Six mutes walked at the head, two by two, carrying black staves and wearing black hatbands. The undertaker, on horseback, followed, preceding eight more horsemen (two conductors, four cloakmen, and two more conductors) riding two by two.

After these came a funeral banner of ostrich feathers and carried by a mute with a page walking on either side. This preceded the hearse, crowned with ostrich feathers supported right and left by Marshal-men in deep mourning and drawn by six black horses. Three mourning coaches, each with its six black horses, followed the hearse, these holding the pall bearers and chief mourners, among whom were noblemen, Members of Parliament, a Cornish contingent which included Sir John St Aubin (sic) and Lord de Dunstanville.

There followed twenty-seven more mourning coaches, each drawn by two horses, filled by eminent artists and friends of the deceased.

Behind these were led the coach of His Highness the Duke of Gloucester; and then twenty-nine more coaches, all with blinds drawn, belonging to various noblemen and gentlemen who had chosen this means of paying tribute to the dead painter. Mrs Opie certainly had reason to be satisfied with the response to her invitations.

Before drawing a blind down over this magnificent funeral attended by many distinguished personages, I must point out that, although it would seem to have been a State funeral, it was evidently not. There is no evidence that Mrs Opie was granted any funds toward it, unlike that of Sir Joshua Reynolds about which Opie as a young man, had said to his sister Betty, 'Aye, girl, and I, too, shall be buried at St Paul's!'

And so it turned out. Opie's reputation stood high enough for him to have the honour of being buried at St Paul's, but it had to be paid for privately. The expense of Sir Joshua's funeral was borne, for their President, by the Academicians, the bill amounting to £588 14s 6d, of which £67 9s was the cost of bands and leather gloves for the servants, and £44 7s 5d the amount of burial fees at St Paul's. As though emphasising disappointment in the lack of the ultimate recognition, Mrs Opie writes in her *Memoir*, 'I bless God that I was *able* to bury him there; nor shall I ever cease to remember with gratitude and satisfaction the long and honourable procession which attended him thither.'

In May 1761, at Mithian in the parish of St Agnes, a fifth child was born to Mary and Edward Opie. His arrival was a mixed blessing to Mary as she was forty-eight years old and felt so embarrassed by its implications that she kept herself indoors to avoid the glances of her fellow-villagers.

However, things did not last long like that for her. Little John Opie captured her heart immediately and was to prove himself the favourite of her five children, so that this late arrival was brought up in an atmosphere of loving care and patient instruction.

Edward, his father, was a carpenter, and a very good one at that. He was, however, a man who worked with his hands and was contemptuous of anyone who thought artists did a man's work. When, therefore, John showed a keenness and an aptitude for drawing, father did nothing to help him pursue it. The boy had also shown himself far beyond the norm in mathematics, and though Edward felt that that, too, was no good for a man to waste his time on, it was not quite so bad as painting.

A story is told of an occasion when a problem of mathematics was to display what was going to be a main feature in Opie's character, namely, dogged perseverance. Ada Earland tells this story of his elder brother and a friend setting him a problem in arithmetic, and making a bet he would be unable to do it.

So difficult was the task that after some days he was no nearer a solution, in spite of determined effort and concentration. One night, when his sister, Betty, had sat up with him until after midnight, he was persuaded by her to give up. He went to bed, sad and dejected.

Two hours later, Betty was awoken by a knock on her door. It was, of course, young John begging for a lighted candle. 'Sister, sister!' he exclaimed. 'I can do it!' Betty gave him a candle, and before she had put something on and followed him downstairs, the boy had finished it off and was jumping around with joy.

At a very early age, probably when he was eleven, Opie's father, Edward, was witness to his son's greater and greater interest in pictures and painting, and in an effort, no doubt, to curb this, what he termed, idleness, he bound him apprentice

to himself. It was while working at some repair work in a
house at which Betty was in service at Mithian that, hanging
on the wall, was a picture of Ellenglaze farmyard which
decided his future career: for he was so affected by this picture
that what till now had been but a vague hope to become an
artist became a purpose, a determination to paint and paint
and paint. But he was still only twelve years old, and still had
his father's contempt to cope with.

The picture hung in the parlour of the house, and young
Opie earned his father's impatient disapproval as time and
again he was seen standing before it, looking at it, drinking the
magic potion in, entranced and excited by this experience of
lively tingling nerves he had never experienced before.

Betty apparently being in service at the house gave her
brother opportunities to return to the vicinity of the picture
which he did many times. A visit to the kitchen always
included a stealthy visit to the parlour and, as soon as he had
memorised aspects of the picture in detail, he hurried back
home to add its message to the picture forming on the canvas
he had been able to obtain. His enthusiasm touched the heart
of the mistress of the house, who, to his disbelief at his good
fortune, allowed him to work on the picture at will. In due
course he had made a good copy of it and sold it for five shillings to Mrs Walker, mother of the vicar of St Winnow, on the
banks of the river Fowey.

'I'm set up for life!' Opie joyously exclaimed to his parents
when he told them the good news. His mother shared his joy,
but predictably his father was not pleased; and for this, given
the manners of the times, one cannot blame him. He himself
was an honest, hard-working craftsman who 'knew his place'
in the social structure, and painting pictures was not for such
as his son who should earn his living in a manner appropriate
to his social position.

One can readily appreciate Edward's disappointment at his
son's ambition, for it was not only in those days that it was
considered that a man should be content to remain in the
station in which God had placed him: for even today, the

ambitious parent is with us who would be horrified if a son was intent on being drawn to the arts. But whereas in Edward's day it was in respect of God's instructions, today it is a case of social pride in materialistic sections of the community.

It was not long, however, before father was won over, and it happened like this.

When mother was in church one Sunday a weary father wanted a nap after reading his Scripture lessons. In the room across the little passage John very quietly arranged his painting materials. He would take advantage of his father's soporific mood and paint his portrait.

At first the unheeding sitter gave John every involuntary assistance, but then Edward showed signs of irritation in his son's increasing excursions into his abode, his staring closely at him, and then walking quickly away again. Annoyed at this trying restlessness on a Sunday afternoon, Edward warned John that if he did it again he would give him a thrashing. He did it again. He had his thrashing, the resulting infusion of sparkle in his father's eyes being just what he wished to paint.

Later, when mother returned home she was struck most favourably by the portrait, not so Edward who was still in two minds about what he should do further to show John his disapproval of his blasphemous use of the Sabbath, but then his eye fell on the picture which mother was holding. He recognised himself immediately, and from then on he glowed with pride showing it to friends and acquaintances, no matter if they were interested or no.

The way was now clear for John to paint and draw, and paint again; but where was he to get the materials from? Chalk, at any rate, was inexpensive and the flat surfaces of walls and horizontals around the house were to become a portrait gallery of the family.

Rather unexpectedly, one might think, Edward at this time decided to cancel his son's apprenticeship with him and he was bound instead to a sawyer, one Mr Wheeler. A sawyer's job was very hard, one man standing in a narrow pit, with the plank to be sawn resting above him, holding the lower end of the saw. The other man of the team, stood above, one leg either side of the pit, and holding the upper handle of the saw. Each then pulled alternately, the blade slowly moving along through the length of the plank, the sawdust smothering the man below.

It is hardly the activity an artist would make his first choice, but it enabled John to pursue his true calling, albeit having to go to bed early in order to devote the early morning to his craft. .

This routine was to last for four years; then, when he was fifteen, a good samaritan arrived on the scene.

Doctor John Wolcot lived in Truro, and besides being a physician, he was a sensitive writer and appreciative of the arts. His list of works occupies over two columns of the *Bibliotheca Cornubiensis.* He was widely travelled, and at one time held the post of Physician General in Jamaica. He was ordained a priest while out there in 1769, and before returning to England in 1773 when he settled in Truro. He wrote under the name of Peter Pindar. This was the man whom fate brought to the cottage at Mithian one day, and who was immediately struck with the drawings there were on every flat surface, drawings of an artist of a strength and vigour that he found quite exceptional. As a result of this visit, which led to further meetings, Opie was presented with an opportunity to leave home and come under the protection of the Truro doctor, ten years older than himself. This was an offer by the physician for him to come and live with him as a protégé and companion. These days such an invitation would raise more than one eyebrow, but there is no doubt that the bizarre relationship was first an intellectual one and only second a role as a companion.

At all events it turned out highly satisfactory for John Opie. Not only was the doctor a well-known literary man, who was also an artist, able to encourage his painting with experience placed at the young man's feet, but also his general education was expanded. His emotions and feelings were nurtured fruitfully and translated into sensitivity for his portraits and other work.

Indeed, Wolcot soon was able to feel justified in recommending Opie to the attention of his patients as a portrait painter and then, in due course, he was invited to paint many subjects by the prestigious families of houses like Tregothnan, Trelowarren, Prideaux Place and St Michael's Mount, yet he was still under eighteen. A detailed, knowledgeable account of this exciting period of Opie's expanding talents can be found in the book I have already mentioned: Earland's *John Opie and his Circle* (Hutchinson, 1911).

During this memoir-making about John Opie, I have no wish to pretend that the story I write owes anything to my own original research. Rather, my pleasure is to present the foregoing book to the attention of my readers, who otherwise might never have heard of it. Indeed, it would be unlikely that anyone other than an historian would come across it, rare as it has now become.

I can only claim to be excused drawing from its voluminous text to the degree I have by virtue of its scholarship and its rarity. My hope is that Ada Earland will have, from her residence now among the spheres, a reason for pleasure that her work is being enjoyed by contemporary readers of this, my humble book.

In 1779, Doctor Wolcot's very individual theories on medicine led to uncomfortable disagreement with both apothecaries and his fellow physicians. His individuality also led him into conflict with the corporation. On his applying to them for another apprentice, he was sent a blatantly unsuitable young man from the Parish Poor list. Wolcot responded to this contrived gesture by writing a letter to the Corporation: 'Gentlemen,' it said, 'Your blunderbuss has missed fire (sic). Yours, John Wolcot.'

He then moved to Helston where he and Opie shared a house in Coinage Hall Street from 1779 to 1782. During that time they visited Plymouth where Wolcot introduced Opie to

William Cookworthy, the discoverer of china-clay in Cornwall. Cookworthy sat for his portrait and, in his *Memoirs of William Cookworthy* gives quite an original description of it:

> It was not his speaking likeness, which would have been all life and fire. It is his thinking likeness, which is very different. And yet, when the rays of the setting sun shed their softened light over the features, as they do for several days, twice in the year, at a late and early period, where the portrait hangs in my present dining room, it is difficult to believe that the countenance to be any but that of a living man in the calm repose of a mighty mind.

It was now, in 1781, that Wolcot tired of the country and, believing that his protégé was now ready to stretch his wings, left Helston and together they went to live in London*. They agreed to share profits, Opie from his pictures and Wolcot from his writing.

They took apartments in Orange Court, Leicester Fields, quite near Sir Joshua Reynolds' Studio, an area just behind what is now the National Gallery. Here John was fired with that excitement of sensing the professional atmosphere, thrilling to the incredible reality that he was living within a few hundred yards of one of the great artists in history, Sir Joshua Reynolds. That was wonder enough for this young man from Cornwall. In no way could he have guessed that Sir Joshua was to say of him, when asked an opinion by another Cornish artist, John Northcote:

'Opie? A wondrous Cornishman who is carrying all before him! He is Caravaggio and Velasquez in one!'

George III had been on the throne twenty-one years when Opie and Wolcot arrived in London, a city that was offsetting the results of the monarch's weakness by extravagant profligacy and corruption. But, on view, above this sordid

*See Appendix E.

state of affairs, Society did its best to make up for his drabness by indulging in ever gayer parties, with libertine undertones and carefree, colourful, tribal rituals. The King was wholly averse to this, setting an example of sobriety, domesticity and frugality that only inspired the party-lovers to ever higher play at the gambling tables, and to an every-increasing consumption of wine. Between the vices of the upper class and the coarse brutality of the lower, the middle class formed a stabilising influence.

This was a time, too, when corruption was at its worst, when Parliamentary seats were openly advertised for sale, and bribes and their acceptance was a normal fact of life [Appendix F].

It was into this spirited world of triviality that John Opie was introduced by his friend, the doctor.

There was, however, another aspect of it, a wind blowing from the heavens and warming the heart, freshening the whole scene of art. Sir Joshua Reynolds was a luminary then, Romney was making four thousand a year, Gainsborough capturing with his brush the beauties of the time.

Stimulating the rich and the not so rich to catch the painter's attention was the fashionable aura such distinguished artists engendered, though their heads were rather too high in the sky for all to feel comfortable in their company.

Earland recounts the arrival of Wolcot and his 'Cornish Wonder' thus:

Into this seething hive of London they came – too blunt, too honest, too indifferent, it would appear, for success where artificiality reigned triumphant. But if the fashionables and wits of Georgian society loved to see their presentiments improved upon, they delighted no less in lion-hunting, and Wolcot knew what he was about when he told his friends that Opie was an untaught genius.

Among others he called on Hearne the engraver, and told him that he had caught a boy in Cornwall with *raw flesh* and that he would take him to his lodgings.

Hearne thought of Opie on first seeing him as 'a rude, clownish boy, with lank, dark hair, and a green feather'. The feather was evidently a ploy of Wolcot's to add to the novelty of this young artist's contrived persona. At all events, almost immediately Opie had his first sitter, and he was followed by a succession of sitters only too anxious to be in the swim of lion-hunting. Here was a strange young man who painted well, and with a Cornish influence so different to the baubles and frippery of London Society, an influence of St Agnes Beacon, westerly gales, and deep holes in the ground where young men were made old at forty.

An opinion of Opie's style at this time comes from a letter that Wolcot wrote to a friend after he had taken Opie to meet the great man, Sir Joshua.

To this friend Colborn, a bookseller, he wrote:

I have again called on Reynolds, President of the Royal Academy, with a pair of John Opie's pictures, the portrait of 'A Jew' and 'A Cornish Beggar', on which he expressed surprise at performances by a boy in a country village containing excellencies that would not disgrace the pencil of Caravaggio. Opie's knowledge of chiaroscuro without ever having seen a picture of the dark masters, drew from his eye a sort of wonder. It strikes me that Reynolds expects Opie to be as perfect in the delineation of the graces as in the heads of vulgar nature, and in consequence become a formidable rival. But here I am sorry to say he will be fortunately mistaken: Opie, I fear, is too fond of imitating coarse expression ... To him, at present, elegance appears affectation, and the forms of Raphael unnatural. He too much resembles a country farmer who, never having tasted anything beyond rough cider, cannot feel the flavour of burgundy or champagne.

Soon after his arrival in London, his friend Northcote came up to London from Plymouth in a third attempt to gain a footing in London as a fashionable portrait painter.

And now, here are two letters concerning an exciting event written at this time. First, one from Wolcot to a friend, John James:

I have at length got Jan [Opie] introduced to the King and Queen – The night before he went I was employed in teaching him how to make King and Queen bows ... As he was carrying his pictures into a room of the Palace, Jan was followed by the Queen, who treated him with great kindness, so much indeed that he is now turned Quixote and is ready to fight up to his knees in blood for her Majesty. The King came in after with a skip: West was with him – I mean West the famous painter, a monstrous favourite of George's – George asked Jan a number of questions which he says he answered with a St Agnes intrepidity. The Queen turned up the whites of her eyes, marvelling, the little Princess lisped praises and Jan, to be sure, was in ecstasies. He remained nearly an hour and a half with 'em, and then took his leave. Of the five pictures he was shown, the King took two, 'The Beggar and his Dog', and the portrait of a lady which Jan had painted especially for him. West was ordered to give Jan the money and to say that he [George III] wished him every success. On Wednesday the boy paints the Duke and Duchess of Gloster (sic), and I suppose the children. He waited on them a few days since and was graciously received by their Royal Highnesses. He is now painting the most beautiful women at the Court, Lady Salisbury, Lady Charlotte Talbot, Lady Harcourt, etc. You can't think what repute the fellow is come into. I told you above I got him introduced: indeed I did, for by recommending him for Mrs Boscawen's patronage, she made it a point to oblige me, and immediately introduced him to Lord and Lady Bute, the Hon and Mrs Walsingham, Lord and Lady Edgcumbe, Mrs Delany, a chief favourite of their Majesties, etc., etc., who showing her picture done by him to the king, he was immediately sent for. Now he is established it will be his own fault if he does not make his fortune.

As I copy the foregoing relation, I get a thrill even now from its substance and a touch from its beam of immediacy telling of the young Cornish boy, from the village of Mithian, honoured by the King and Queen of England two hundred years ago.

And if I can feel this from that long distance, I wonder how Edward, his father, reconciled it with his early disdain for the art his son was to follow.

Edward received the news in a letter, dated 11th March 1782, to his mother written in so delightfully casual a manner that father might be forgiven if he had not taken it in.

The King and Queen do not come first in his news, but rather his regret at hearing his brother has been poorly and giving him advice. Then this letter to his mother goes on:

> I have all the prospect of success that is possible having much more business than I can possibly do. I have been with the King and Queen who were highly pleased with my works, and took two of my pictures, and they are hung up in the King's collection at the Queen's Palace ...
>
> There is no work stirring at this time, and it is a very improper time to see the town as it is cold and very dirty, and so full of smoak and fog that you can hardly see the length of your nose and I should not be able to stir out anywhere by day nor keep them indoors nor keep them company indoors [referring to Betty's plans] by reason of the quantity of business I would advise them to come up in June when they may see everything in fine weather, and probably I shall not be so busy as I am now, because most of the quality go out of town at that time and then also they may see all the great houses etc., but now the families are in town, they'd not be able to see one. As to my stay here, it will depend on circumstances, as to the continuation of employ and the encouragement I may meet with. If I have time I shall certainly come down in the summer.
>
> Many have been in town years and have had nothing to

do, whilst I who have been here but two or three months, am known and talked of by everybody. To be known is the great thing in London. A man may do ever so well, if nobody knows, it will signify nothing, and among so many thousands of people it is no easy matter to get known.

I cannot resist invoking the aid of Earland again to help me with a description of the fashionable world Opie now found himself in. I cannot claim any authentic knowledge of it; but just see what she makes of it:

How the inward eye luxuriates in visions of lace-ruffled society of George III's earlier years! After our utilitarian attire, even the sober-hued cloth, laced with gold or silver, of everyday wear is picturesque: the delicately tinted satins and velvets of state occasions must have furnished a riot of colours. Masculine attire was still beautiful when Opie came to London, although there was a growing tendency to sobriety of colour. The sword was still an essential part of a gentleman's outfit – not merely for ornament unfortunately; for although duelling was illegal, he would have been a brave man who dared refuse a challenge. Life then had leisure for courtly interchange of compliments; fans fluttered furtive messages under the very eyes of watchful chaperones. The attraction of the past lies in externals; our mind's eye recreates the glittering throng, but is conveniently blind to the absence of all our comfort and decency.

As the day wanes, many of the gentlemen who visit Opie's studio show too evident an over-indulgence in wine – a condition accepted by the ladies with an indifference which proves it too ordinary an occurrence to excite remark or disgust. Paint, powder and patches are ineffectual to conceal the ravages of smallpox or the havoc wrought by nights at the gaming table. We are too accustomed to well-paved and lighted streets to appreciate them. Could we go back to Opie's day we should find that the coaches and

sedan chairs wait outside his studio in a street inches deep
in mud and garbage; where pedestrians walked warily
along a narrow, kerbless, ill-paved footway, usually only
wide enough for one. At each step they could be splashed
from head to foot with noisome mud from the gutter, with
oil from the ineffectual lamps that glimmered outside the
shops and houses. There were other perils, too, on the
homeward way. Highwaymen and footpads abounded,
little wonder that they should when the citizens had to rely
on watchmen who were apparently chosen for their
decrepitude and senility as fit guardians of the King's
lieges.

Beyond Hyde Park the traveller looked to his pistols, and
on Sunday evenings a kind of convoy was organised by
means of a bell tolling in Kensington so that visitors who
had to return to the city might assemble and travel in
company for mutual protection. In the same year that Opie
came to London, the famous Horace Walpole, and Lady
Browne, were robbed by a single highwayman, neither
were injured, but Lady Browne was terrified he would
somehow find her, for she had given him her purse with
only bad money in it which she regularly carried for that
purpose.

'Prepare for death,' wrote Dr Johnson in 1782, 'if here at night
you roam, And sign your will before you sup from home.'

As one who experienced in 1980 an attack in the Strand in
London at 11.30 p.m. at night, it is reasonable for me to put
forward the cliché, Plus ça change ...

Opie had arrived in London in the autumn of 1781. He was
only twenty-one years old, yet he had during that winter been
the most sought after and lionised portrait painter in London.
This was in part due to the refreshing contrast of the attraction of his solid peasant figure and his uncompromising figure
of speech, a blunt charm set against the general foppery of
London Society at that time. Though he painted several
excellent portraits, curiously enough he exhibited none in the

Royal Academy Exhibition that summer of 1782. Instead, he had five pictures hung: 'A Country Boy and Girl', 'An Old Woman', 'An Old Man's Head', 'A Beggar in Armenian Dress', and 'Boy and Dog'. Opie's recent notoriety ensured that his pictures were a centre of attraction. His exhibits ensured that he upheld his reputation as being the Wonder of the Year.

Two misfortunes now occurred that were to cause Opie to change the direction of the comparatively even tenor of his ways, the stability of his friendship with the more worldly Wolcot, and the security the continued demand from would-be sitters to have their portrait painted.

The first event was due to Opie meeting the daughter of a solicitor, who was also a money-lender, named Benjamin Bunn, of St Botolphs, Aldgate. Mr Bunn had a bevy of attractive daughters of whom one, Mary, appealed especially to Opie. She was attractive and pretty and soon Opie was in love with her. She responded, though cynics might say that Mr Bunn saw in the 21-year-old, lionised artist, a catch for his daughter that would not be repeated.

At all events, Opie resolved to marry her, forgetting the girl left behind in Mithian, Mary James, whose portrait (unfinished) was found years later when he died and his effects were being sold. Though it is not certain, it was thought that she was the model in this life-size painting of a girl in the dairy, milking. The picture was sold for £2.00.

The marriage took place on 4th December 1782, in St Martin-in-the-Fields, which seems very grand. The witnesses were 'Benjamin and M Bunn'. There was no sign of Wolcot.

Mary was a bright young girl who was sadly misled by her father's enthusiasm and Opie's infatuation, for they had absolutely nothing in common on which a marriage could be expected to last, not least in that Opie's number one, all consuming interest was his painting, and anything of himself he could give a wife was very meagre. That being said, it was not until twelve years had passed before Mary left Opie and went off with another man.

The marriage led to the second misfortune he suffered, for, when he took his wife to live in Orange Court, it caused friction between Wolcot and Opie, and opened up to view the trouble that had been silently brewing between the two men, namely, the fact that the bargain that they would share gains equally was now very unequal, Wolcot's earnings from his writing being much less than that of Opie. The split was made amicably and the two men remained friends.

His second wife, Amelia, whom we shall meet formally later on, wrote a memoir about her husband after his death, and this was published together with material from the series of important lectures on art and painting which he had delivered to his Fellow Academicians, incidentally a great honour for the Cornishman.

In the memoir on her husband, Amelia gave short shrift to her predecessor, Mary; but she does unwittingly give us an idea of what Mary had to put up with as wife of a famous artist.

There follows a brief summary of what emerges from Amelia's experience:

Opie was a man of exceptional mental powers. Brilliant in congenial society he was prey to fits of morose silence and despondency. He was almost totally absorbed in his work. He spent long hours in his painting-room (sic) from half-past-eight in summer, and there he virtually remained painting until half-past-four in winter and five in summer.

When Opie emerged from this session, a young wife might expect to go out with him, to a masquerade, for example, at Vauxhall, or to the play-house; but no, Opie spent his evenings studying or reading, until bed-time, great books of instruction, or studying prints of the ancient and modern masters, or sketching designs of various descriptions.

Another cross that Mary had to bear (as did Amelia later) was Opie's attention to economy. However affectionate he might have been this phobia for not spending was bound to be the cause of friction. A young wife understandably would jib at having to settle for this life style when she well knew that the money was coming in fast. But Opie was no miser. He had experienced poverty and he had seen how little dependence could be placed on a continuance of prosperous days.

From a comfortable distance of two centuries, it is fun to see that the housewife then had very similar problems to the housewife today.

In 1795 there was not only a war on, but a bad harvest as well. Shortage of wheat led to riots in many parts of the country, Cornwall not excepted. Pastry and puddings were given up in many private houses to save flour, and a letter-writer in *The Times* suggested that no soup should be made in well-off houses as so much meat, which would have relieved poor families, is wasted.

On butchers' stalls alongside the prices of food stuffs were displayed [converted to our modern currency] thus:

Prices of Provisions		*Journeymen's Wages*	
Mutton	5p a lb.	Carpenters	60p per week
Lamb	5½p a lb.	Shoemakers	50p per week
Veal	5½p a lb.	Bakers	45p per week
Beef	6p a lb.	Gardeners	40p per week
Small Beer	10p a quart	Smiths	40p per week
Bread	5p a loaf	Husbandmen	35p per week

You may care to hear of this latterday recession in a little more detail.

Hair powder, for instance, was taxed for the first time, and in July the King set an example of economy by ordering that the Royal Household, including his own table, should be supplied only with bread made from a mixture of wheaten flour and rye, or wheat and potatoes.

Travelling charges were affected, too. The charge for travelling 'post' i.e. in post chaises, was raised from the equivalent of our modern currency of 5p a mile to 6p.

Such restrictions as these in everyday life have their effect on tempers from time to time and domestic tensions are not improved by them; so that they may have had a place in bringing the imbalance of the marriage to a head. Poor Mary, she was a young woman who needed affectionate attention, and marrying an artist, both popular as a man and as an artist was not the most probable way to get it. Northcote who, you remember, was Opie's friend (sometimes a jealous one) and an artist said that with a different husband Mary Opie might have made a good wife. She had a 'mild feeling disposition', and Opie was no more fitted to be married than a log of wood. He had none of the softness fit for married life. Opie was the greatest man he ever saw – and the greatest devil.

Included in this stricture could have been the manner of his disengaging from the marriage, though once a decision is made that all is over there cannot be anything but pain and regret in the hearts of both parties: and the way the final break is made is bound to hurt, if only because of the sad sense of waste and failure after so much effort to keep alight dying embers.

The Opie marriage break-up was no different to the many in which one partner tires before the other, and it must have been hell for Mary and wretched for him. In an effort to escape from the *ennui* of an unhappy home life, Opie began to see a lot of a man called Edward Beetham, who was a bright and stimulating character, versatile and inventive, who lived with his wife in Fleet Street. Fleet Street was then the business centre for booksellers, publishers and engravers. He was from the North, from Westmorland, a county which stifled his energies at an early age, so he ran away from home and his Puritan father, joined a travelling theatrical company and eventually drifted to London and Fleet Street where he became a publisher. He was also something of an inventor with the restless instincts of a modern day entrepreneur; in fact a man, should Opie meet such a one in the street, who would certainly delight him.

This proved to be the case, but another member of the family was to prove to be the pull. Edward Beetham had an attractive wife and was a painter. She was energetic, generous, hospitable and independent of the power of convention that smothered life in Society. She was also a mother, and her eldest daughter Jane had inherited her mother's artistic tastes and her father's wit and energy. She was also attractive in a manner that was apparent at any gathering at which she might find herself.

Opie agreed to give Jane lessons in painting, thus ensuring a developing propinquity dangerous when one party is a very attractive and talented young woman and the other is in the prime of life and unhappily married. However, the lessons went on with mutual satisfaction, Jane having four of her pictures hung in the Royal Academy Exhibition of 1794.

It was apparent to all the visitors to the studio that Opie was more and more enchanted by Jane, who became a cause for the studio to become rather like a salon in which interesting people gathered, enjoying each other's company, while Mary Opie was left by her husband to her own resources.

After a while Mary, humiliated by her husband's inattention, began to look elsewhere. She found that many of those who came to the studio were men who clearly encouraged her to realise she could benefit herself by joining in and responding to their attention.

In due course one of these, an older man, a Major Edwards, who was persistent in his attentions, made Mary feel he filled the emptiness in her heart, gave her the warmth of a man's love, the comfort of being wanted again.

One morning in May 1795 Mary gently closed the front door behind her, having told the housekeeper she was dining with her father. She left no other message, and it was not until two or three days had passed that a note was delivered to the house informing Opie that she was at Clifton with Major Edwards, and that she would not be coming back.

That evening Northcote called on Opie and found him looking very glum. To his revelation that his wife had left him, Northcote replied that that was nothing more than he had long expected.

After prolonged, tedious and expensive exposure to lawyers during the next two years, Opie was granted a divorce, Mary making no attempt to defend. Mary married Major Edwards forthwith. While there is a notion that the marriage was not altogether a success, the major left her comfortably provided for when he died; but poor Opie was to suffer another domestic setback, for as soon as the divorce was through he asked Jane's father for his daughter's hand; and the request was refused. In the imperious manner of fathers of this period he exercised his rights and saw that she was married to a rich, eccentric, elderly suitor, John Read, of Maddox Street.

During all this period of domestic upset for Opie, his work continued to impress and to remain in demand. Only the commissions for portraits did not sustain their former demand. However, this reduction freed him to broaden his scope and he turned to creating large paintings of historical, dramatic events, enthusiasm for which was then in vogue, and his reputation lost none of its status. Two canvases, the 'Death of Rizzio' (1787) and 'The Assassination of James I of Scotland' (1787) are two paintings of this time which made considerable impact, and which led to his receiving the honour of being elected an Associate of the Royal Academy.

This is as good a place as any to record here the summary of works Opie painted, which is a clear indication of the scope of his subjects. This list is taken from Jope Rogers' *Opie and his Works*:

Portraits (counting each head in family groups	508
Sacred subjects	22
Historical	17
Shakespeare	11
Poetical and Fancy	134
Landscape	5
Various	63
	760

No less than 143 pictures were hung at the Royal Academy.

A broken marriage is a defeat for each, the end of a period of effort on either side to save the union that started out so well, to which much love and care had been bestowed. One of the parties will care more than the other, but each will suffer something he or she never expected, the gap left by the sudden flight of habit that leaves in its place barren time, barren purpose.

Opie, occupied with his commissions and in personal contact with his sitters, was lucky in this respect, but no doubt he spent many an hour at night regretting his failure to fulfil the hopes of Mary Bunn. He was, fortunately, not to wait long before fate opened another door. Jane Beetham was eclipsed and Amelia Alderson came on the scene.

Amelia was everything that Mary was not – vivacious, gay, clever, and a writer of poetry and a novel before she was eighteen. She also wrote highly dramatic plays. Yet she was accomplished, too, always the life and soul of a party. She loved society, and acting, and singing. She was very popular with a string of admirers by whom she had remained unconquered. She was, in fact, as different to John Opie as could be imagined, she a vivacious extrovert, he a tense introvert.

Miss Alderson had, too, her choice of suitors from high society with any one of which she could have made what is called a very good match, but her head was always the arbiter of her adventures, and her heart kept subservient until the one and only arrived who could quicken her pulse with its undeniable and wholly recognisable message.

One evening Opie was at a party when he found himself alone with an elderly gentleman, who interspersed their conversation with frequent references to the fact that, 'Where is Amelia, she should be here by now' or 'I'm sure I'm not mistaken, she *is* coming, she must be here soon …' Opie found this rather distracting, certainly he did not share the old gentleman's anticipatory pleasure, indeed, the reverse was the case.

But then … then Opie saw the door open and in its frame there stood a ravishing creature. 'Who's that? Who is it?' he exclaimed, abruptly, to no one in particular. The new arrival, after pausing for a moment, hurried in, expectant enthusiasm on her face, all brightness and smiles and animation, eager to greet her friends.

She had abundant hair of a rich auburn hanging in waved tresses over her shoulders. Her blue dress left her white neck and arms bare, and on her head was perched on one side a coquettish bonnet, made to look even smaller than it was by a plume of three white feathers.

John Opie fell for her immediately, and in a big way, and thus began the happiest years of his life. One would like to think that his rapture was acknowledged with music, songs sung by Miss Amelia Alderson who also had a fine soprano voice to add to her accomplishments. We can savour a link with her this present day for one of the favourite songs she used to sing was 'Sally in our Alley'.

It so happens that Southey, the poet, described Opie as he saw him at this time; and here, by Southey, is the man that Amelia had conquered that evening:

> Opie is indeed a very extraordinary man. I have now twice seen him. Without anything of politeness, his manners are pleasing, though their freedom is out of the common: and his conversation, though in a half-uttered, half-Cornish, half croak, is interesting.
>
> There is a strange contrast between his genius which is not confined to painting, and the vulgarity of his appearance, – his manners, and sometimes his language. You will, however, easily conceive that a man who can paint like Opie must display the same taste on other subjects.

Amelia was the daughter of a doctor, a widower now, in Norwich, and throughout her happy marriage to Opie ruthlessly, one might say, spent long periods in her home town while Opie, though he longed for her to return to London, wisely let her have as long a rein as she liked.

This happy meeting took place in the spring of 1797, and they were married at Marylebone Church on 8th May 1798.

Opie took her to his house, No 8 Berners Street, where the remained for the rest of his life.

There is no doubt that the marriage to the popular Amelia revitalised his attraction to Society as a portrait painter, and during the years 1799 and 1800 he had a constant succession of sitters, one of them being Charlotte, the Princess Royal.

Amelia's happy outlook on life had its counterpart in her morbid interest in crime and violence. One of the major attractions for her in Norwich were the Assizes. At first sight this might seem somewhat strange, especially as her interest extended to all that was grim in the criminal world; but then her sensibilities were bound to be drawn in many directions seeing that her natural instinct was to feed her inquiring mind as a novelist.

Opie did everything to encourage her writing, and this interest and support must have been a major ingredient in the happy marriage which lasted in its romantic state for ten years, until his death.

The work load of Opie, meanwhile, was causing her some anxiety, and in her memoir of him she recounts how hard and tiresome life is for a fashionable portrait painter. Sitters were exacting, his detractors accusing him of meeting those comments that levelled any criticism of the likeness, with coarse plainess of speech.

Of all employments, portrait-painting is perhaps the most trying to a man of pride and sensibility [she writes] and the most irritating to an irritable man. To hear beauties and merits in a portrait often stigmatised as deformities and blemishes: to have high lights taken for white spots and dark effective shadows for the dirty appearance of a snuff-taker: to witness discontent to the standers-by because the painting does not exhibit the sweet smile of the sitter, though it is certain that a smile on canvas looks like the grin of idiocy; while a laughing eye ...

Persons of worship, as Mr Opie used to call them, that is, persons of great consequence, either from talent, rank or widely spreading connections, are sometimes attended by others whose aim is to endeavour to please the great man or woman by flattery, wholly at the expense of the poor artist; and to minister sweet food to the palate though it be wormwood to that of the painter ...

... My temper and patience has so often been on the point of deserting me even when Mr Opie had not, apparently, undergone the slightest alteration – a strong proof that he possessed some of that self-command which is one of the requisites of good breeding, but it is certain that the picture suffered on such occasions ...

Amelia, intelligent and articulate, and a born chatterer, was no respecter of fools; and one can imagine the atmosphere in the studio when she was all but boiling over with contempt and anger at a sitter's vapid opinions of her husband's work.

Amelia, with her talents and popularity, her gaiety and the fact that she was an only child, could so easily have made her spoilt, particularly as Opie was one who preferred to stay at home except for an opportunity to meet people who provided good conversation. In such company he was at his best, and there is a story about that great actress, Mrs Siddons, to illustrate this asset.

At a party one evening, Mrs Siddons asked, 'And where is Mr Opie? I heard he was to be here.'

'He is gone.'

'I am sorry for it,' she replied, 'for I meant to have sought him out, as when I am with him I am always sure to hear him say something which I cannot forget, or at least which ought never to be forgotten.'

A major reason for the success of this marriage, an extremely happy marriage, was the tolerance for, and encouragement given, to each of the two to continue with their natural inclinations, he for the more serious forms of entertainment, and she the more flippant and the gayer. However, in doing this, as I have already said, she did not suffer fools gladly.

This young, entertaining, and pretty wife of Opie's was, however, destined to carry in her heart the weight of that misfortune that God, in His wisdom and for His own mysterious plan, imposes on a woman: Amelia longed for a child that had always been in her dreams but which she was never called upon to bear.

While she and Opie were staying with her father in 1801/2 her maternal desires welled up to the extent of her suggesting to Opie that they should adopt a child, and one whom she already had in mind. The child was a little girl called Eleanor Rooks, the daughter of a Norwich architect. The mother refused. She could not bear to part with the child who was about six years old.

'Then,' said Opie, 'I must paint her.'

For her sitting she was put into a smart white frock which was elaborately worked.

'Has she no other dress?' asked Opie. The nurse replied yes, she had a blue and a white gingham.

'Then put on the blue.'

His rather forbidding welcome soon changed to one of pleasure for, rather unexpectedly Amelia thought, children were soon put at their ease in the painting room and were allowed to run around in a very free manner.

In 1803, a vigorous figure in London political life was a radical clergyman named John Horne Tooke. His extreme politics were so objectionable to the Government that a special act was passed to unseat him, though it was presented in general terms to disqualify anyone in Holy Orders for a seat in Parliament. This act is still on the Statute Book today.

I bring the reverend gentleman into our circle so that we can learn what such an unpopular kind of fellow thought of Opie.

During the sittings Tooke had ample opportunity to assess Opie's status as a conversationalist. His verdict was, 'Mr Opie crowds more wisdom into a few words than any man I ever knew; he speaks, as it were, in axioms, and what he observes is worthy to be remembered.'

That summer Mrs Opie, as usual, spent a long time away in Norwich, much to the chagrin of her husband, for she was staying away longer than had been agreed. He urged her to return:

> My affection for you is ever increased in point of general feeling and interest, so that if I do not admire you more, I feel you more a part of myself than I ever did at first ... Let me hear on Wednesday how you are. The cat and parrot are both well, and the kitten beautiful and merry. The guns have been firing today, but on what account I am ignorant yet.
>
> Adieu my only love.

In the summer of 1805, Opie and his wife had a lengthy stay in Norwich. He had been working very hard and prudence induced him to stay with Amelia far away from his painting room and its servitude.

He wrote to Davies Giddy (later President of the Royal Society) a letter at this time which gives a picture of this holiday's ingredients.

> ... I have been spending some five weeks at Norwich, and parts adjacent, where, through the medium of beef, dumplings, wine, riding, swimming, walking and laughing, I have endeavoured (I hope not unsuccessfully) to lay in a stock of vigour against winter; and my time, I must say, has passed pleasantly enough, as in addition to the above-mentioned substantial and capital enjoyments, I have occasionally had some agreeable conversation with several not unclever people ...

The winter's work that followed was heavy, and included no less than eighteen portraits, including one of the poet Southey; and then, in the summer that followed, the Opies were asked to stay in a grand house, that of Mr Whitbread at Southill, near Biggleswade. A letter that Amelia sent to her father extolling this visit gives us an attractive picture of a country house party of the time.

They arrived at Southill at three in the afternoon which was three hours before they were expected and so no one was in. After being taken to their rooms (sic) and 'by the time the sandwiches sent to them were eaten', Mr Whitbread and the family had returned from their drive. The host must have had reason to have Opie to himself for he was 'carried off' by his host in the barouche while Amelia went a walk with one of the guests.

At six, we all met at dinner and I need not tell you our dinner was excellent. The only guests are [Sir Joshua] Reynolds, Wilkie [a rising young painter] and Lady Roslyn and her children. After a pleasant evening, Lady Elizabeth [Whitbread] being much recovered, we retired at eleven, and were summoned to meet the next morning at the breakfast table at nine that we might get off for Woburn Abbey in good time.

We got away a little before eleven, Tom Adkin and Wilkie in a gig, Lady Elizabeth Whitbread, Lady Roslyn, Miss Whitbread, her brother, Reynolds and ourselves in the barouche and four greys, driven by Mr Whitbread. The day was only too fine, as its extreme brightness almost made it impossible to gaze on the really pretty country which we passed.

During their stay there was a very violent thunderstorm. No one was down yet and Opie stood under the colonnade. There was violent forked lightning, and Amelia watched him, fascinated by the violence of the storm which, after a little more time, began to frighten her until she thought she was going to faint.

With this, perhaps, in mind, she wrote of this storm and commented that 'no society and no situation, however honourable, however pleasant, could long keep him from his studio'.

Never did I see him so happy, when absent from London, as he was there, for he felt towards his host and hostess every sentiment of respect and admiration which it is pleasant to feel and honourable to inspire. But though he was the object of the kindest and most flattering attention he sighed to return to London and his pursuits: and when he had been at Southill only eight days, he said to me, on my expressing my unwillingness to go away, 'Though I shall be ever anxious to come hither again, recollect that I have been idle *eight days*'.

During that time, Opie painted a number of quick portraits of his host, but his referring to the 'idle' days implies that none were commissions.

Amelia went on to Norwich to make it a longer holiday until his appealing and despondent letters began to worry her. Poor Opie, he began to regret his indulgence in letting her know of this loneliness, and we find him writing:

My dearest life, I cannot be sorry that you do not stay longer; though, as I said, on your father's account, I would consent to it. Pray, love, forgive me, and make yourself easy, for I did not suspect, until my last letter was gone that it might be too strong: I had been counting almost the hours till your arrival for some time, and have been unwell and unable to sleep these last three weeks so that I could not make up my mind to the disappointment. As to coming down again, I cannot think of it; for though I could, perhaps, better spare the time at present from painting than I could at any part of last month, I find I now must go hard at work to finish my lectures.

Opie had received the honour of being elected Professor of Painting at the Royal Academy, and this bound him to give a course of six lectures to his colleagues and favoured guests. Such a task would be very demanding on anyone not accustomed to lecturing, but to prepare such a course on their own subject to his fellow Academicians must have been both onerous and intimidating in the extreme. It is to this course of lectures that he is referring above in his letter. Opie goes on:

> The law says they must be delivered the second year after election, and though they have never acted on this law, yet there are many, perhaps, who would be glad to put it in force in the present instance. I had almost given way to the suggestions of idleness, and determined to put them off for another year; but since I have been acquainted with the above-mentioned regulation I have shut myself up in the evenings and, I doubt not, shall be ready with three or four of them at least ...
>
> Pray, love, be easy, and as (I suppose) you will not stay; come up as soon as possible, for I long to see you as much as ever I did in my life.

The lectures, or 'Discourses' as they were called, were delivered before the Royal Academy in 1807, and each was a major success. Four were on the practical aspect of the subject of painting, namely, 'Design or Drawing', 'Colouring', 'Chiaroscuro', and 'Composition'. Two considered it from the intellectual point of view, namely 'Invention' and 'Expression'. To give an idea of the fine style of Opie's lectures, I will extract a short piece he delivered on colour. The series is of the same high standard – beautifully expressed, and clearly pictured:

> Colour, the peculiar object of the most delightful of our senses, is associated in our minds with all that is rare, precious, delicate, and magnificent in nature. A fine complexion is the dye of love and the hint of something celestial: the ruby, the rose, the diamond, the youthful blush, the orient morning, and the variegated splendour of the setting sun, consist of, or owe their charms principally to colour.
>
> To the sight it is the index of gaiety, richness, warmth and animation; and should the most experienced artist, by

design alone, attempt to render the eternal freshness of spring the fervid vivacity of summer, or the mellow abundance of autumn, what must be his success?

Colouring is the sunshine of art, that clothes poverty in smiles rendering the prospect of bareness itself agreeable, while it heightens the interest and doubles the charm of beauty.

While delivering these lectures he was still very busy with commissions, though he had come to feel tired and lacking his usual vigour after this heavily engaged winter of 1806/7. Even so, no one close to him expected that his end was near when he gladly accepted another royal commission, a portrait of the Duke of Gloucester. This was to prove one of his finest works, the background being finished by his friend Thompson while he himself lay dying on his sick-bed.

Just before this, the editor of *The Artist* asked him to contribute an article by a given date. He replied, 'I am tired of writing, and I mean to be a gentleman during the spring months and keep a horse, and ride every evening.' But the decision to slow down was made too late.

Within a few days of delivering his lecture on colour he caught a cold that soon developed into a fever which became worse rapidly, and it became apparent he was seriously ill. A day or so later Betty, his sister, arrived to share the nursing with Amelia. Doctors were in regular attendance coming three and four times a day. Advice from a consultant surgeon was also sought.

On 10th April, Southey was informed by William Taylor, of Norwich, and a close friend of both the Opies, that 'Mr Opie has been at the point of death from abdominal paralysis which, Doctor Sayer says, may reasonably be classed as the Devonshire Colic, and ascribed to the absorption of the lead vapours to which plumbers and painters often fall victims.'

There is no record of the doctors' opinions except that it was a 'slow consuming illness'. In the Annual Register of 1807 his death was ascribed to 'an inflammation of the brain'.

Fortunately, he was not many days suffering, for on Thursday, 9th April 1807, at about four o'clock in the afternoon, he turned his face to the wall, and died.

*

At the Royal Institution of Cornwall (in Truro) there are several fine paintings by Opie on view. All are portraits, beautifully painted. I found myself there one morning looking at the exquisite brushwork of the eyes of a girl from whose face, only a few inches from mine there suddenly emanated an extraordinary aura of truth. I could not believe this girl was not with me now; don't I feel her breath on my cheek?

And then I realised I was looking intimately at Opie's paintwork with my eye positioned in the very place where his eye led him to decide that 'Yes that is it. I cannot do it any better'. I was with Opie. Opie was with me.

And two centuries of time had spun away.

VIII

The Great Trevithick

Spray has given me a delightful night's rest. Hove-to, as she has been, has meant she has had no way on her; nevertheless I am now in the cockpit five hours after I set the sails last night and we've drifted with the flood tide coming up channel, till we've got where we are now, past the Dodman, past Fowey and just about abreast of Looe Island.

Mind you, she couldn't have behaved herself so adroitly (for we are making for Rame Head) if the wind had changed direction. Five or six times during the night, I put my head up through the cabin hatch to check position and see whether there was any traffic, but all was under control and the moonlight visibility was as clear as daylight, so that there was no risk involved.

At one point in the night, I wanted to check something I had on my mind and I stretched my hand up to the bookshelf that ran along the length of the bunk to get down the *Pilot*. In doing so, I dislodged something and it fell down onto my pillow. It was my passport, which I always have with me onboard to enable me to take advantage of any whim I might have to call in at a French port. Seeing it, there suddenly occurred to me that it might not still be valid and I flicked over a page to see the date – but all was well. I had another four weeks.

One doesn't often look properly at one's passport but I found myself looking at my name *Nigel Trevithick Tangye*. That name *Trevithick* – my word! I remembered, as a child at school far, far away from Cornwall I was unaware of what a proud name it was, and only prayed that *no one* would ask me what the 'T' in the middle of 'N.T.T.' stood for. From such inconsequential things can the young secretly suffer.

Soon we shall be meeting this famed Richard Trevithick whose name I am now justly proud to bear. Indeed, I have other links with this giant of a man who was also one of the greatest engineers in history. And if, by chance, reader of mine, you are one of those who flinch at the prospect of trying to be interested in an 'engineer', bear with me and I believe you will change your mind. For one thing, he was a giant of a man inventing and designing large machines in heavy engineering. It was he, for example, who invented the prototype steam engine railway locomotive, and the first travelling carriage which needed no horse, its first trip carrying passengers being up Beacon Hill in Camborne. Well that's not a bad start, is it, the forerunner of the railway train and the 'motor' car?

With his discovery of new principles of engineering employing the use of steam, he vastly improved the efficiency of the mines in Cornwall so that he had the esteem and gratitude of the county, and the admiration of those others who contributed toward the wondrous engineering achievements of the nineteenth-century Industrial Revolution.

And that is why I had to suffer my middle name, Trevithick, for my grandfather was just such a disciple and, with three of his brothers, built up an engineering business that was known all over the world. Trevithick died within a few weeks of my grandfather being born (1831/2). Further associations contributed to my being a devotee: the Tangye brothers had their home in Illogan [*vide* my *The Living Breath of Cornwall*] and so had Trevithick. Finally, by golly, I was a Founder Member and Vice-Chairman of the Trevithick Society formed in the fifties and flourishing today.

Thinking on these things on this fine summer morning in *Spray* I find my sense of well-being has become clouded by the picture of a small group of three or four ships a mile out to seaward from *Spray* and sailing in the opposite direction. The year is 1810 and we are at war with France and one of these vessels is a Falmouth packet ship in convoy, having just escaped from a chase by a French man-of-war: on board is Trevithick, ill and worn out, with his long-suffering wife who has saved his life with her nursing. He cannot be anything but terribly depressed, fate being for the time being against him, but he will be home six days after leaving London and his beloved mother will be there to welcome them. This was not to be; he was to find that she had just died, and only a short while before his arrival.

*

To put it simply, what follows is about one of the greatest engineers there has ever been.

Richard Trevithick was born on 13th April 1771, in the parish of Illogan in the family home, a cottage at the foot of the north west slope of Carn Brea. It was almost in the centre of the area embracing the richest Cornish mines – Dolcoath, Cook's Kitchen, Pool, Tin Croft, and Roskear. Not one was more than a mile away. He was a man of the people, prolific in ingenuity and energy and imagination.

He was the first son of five children and was his mother's favourite. She was a large, friendly woman whose wedding ring was seven-eighths of an inch diameter and engraved, 'God above, increase our love'.

Shortly after his birth the family moved house to Penponds, near Camborne, where he went to school. His report at term-end described him as a disobedient, slow, obstinate, spoiled boy, frequently absent and very inattentive.

His school subjects were limited to reading, writing and arithmetic, drawing from the latter the remark that 'Your sum may be right, but it is not done by the rule', to which the boy replied, 'I'll do six sums to your one'.

His father, captain of the prestigious Dolcoath Mine, and a most respected one at that, wanted his son to sit at an office desk but he chose to meander through the entrails of the mines himself, keeping to himself.

A problem that arose among a group of mine agents about

some underground levels led the young Trevithick to offer to help solve the difficulty. At first, heads were shaken in silence, but then, not meeting with success themselves, they allowed him to try his hand. His as yet undetected genius enabled him to recognise an incompatibility between a magnetic needle and adjoining iron elements and there was no longer any problem for the older hands.

The first time we hear of him being employed in a mine was in 1779 when he was eighteen, but by then he must have absorbed enough of the industrial flavour in this central mining area to have worked in many aspects of it. All day, and night, too, black smoke was billowing overhead like mushrooms whose storks were the tall chimneys we are so aware of today; and reminding us of this era in the 18th/19th century when Cornwall was an industrial region of England.

The coal had to be imported, also raw material like iron. This was, for example, for the boilers, and these plates had to be made small (even for huge boilers) because of the awful, narrow roads along which no heavy wheeled traffic was practicable. Such imports had to be transported from the port to the mines on the backs of mules; they would be herded thirty or forty at a time, one behind the other to an accompaniment of raucous shouts of command, *ad lib*, by the 'conductors' of the long string of animals, hauling their ponderous load along the rutted pool-filled roads.

It is safe to say that Trevithick spent long hours in the engine houses for it was in them that the great engines kept the workings free of water which, were it not for the pumps, would be drowned. The steam pumping engine was to a mine what the heart is to a man.

At the time we are considering, the boiler of the mine engine had to be fed with vast amounts of coal. It was to be this young lad of eighteen who was going to be the engineering magician that developed a new principle of steam power that the whole world was going to be grateful for.

We hear of him the following year being employed at Stray Park mine at a salary of 30s a month. He had acquired an admiration locally for his prodigious strength and also for being startlingly quick at mental arithmetic. Great feats began to be recorded of him. He could lift half a ton. As a wrestler he had no equal in Cornwall. He could throw a ball over the tower of Camborne church while standing close enough to the base to touch it with his foot. He climbed the mine shears, which reached up over the shaft some sixty feet high (the shaft going some thousand feet deep) and stood at their peak swinging a sledgehammer and balancing his huge form apparently with no fear for his safety at all.

At a mine-account supper, conviviality led to an altercation with a Captain Hodge who challenged Trevithick to a wrestling match: in a flash the challenger found himself hoisted up, turned upside down so that his feet hit the ceiling. For many years the boot marks could be seen on the ceiling, telling evidence of his strength. It was due to events like the foregoing that he came to be known as the 'Cornish Giant'.

He really was a remarkable figure of a man, with his stunning physique, with his bright, keen, light-blue eyes. Fair complexioned, he had a clear, ruddy skin, and his expression revealed kindness and tolerance. A personality of strong appeal, he was nevertheless easily elated or depressed.

Perhaps I should give a brief resume of the history behind the mine engines that Trevithick was to create and improve during his lifetime. Put like that, it may sound dull to my patient reader, but it will take only a few lines to give the gist.

The first steam pumping engine used for pumping out volumes of endlessly encroaching water from the mine workings in which the metal lodes were situated was erected in 1702. This was much improved by Newcomen, and in turn, successive generations of Cornish engineers followed with further improvements. Jonathan Hornblower was another. The chief difficulty they met with was inability to provide sufficient power to keep the mines safe and dry, once pumped dry, and to find a means of reducing the very extravagant consumption of coal which first had to be shipped from the mines in Wales. That was the situation when Trevithick had grown to manhood.

One of his first inventions was when he perfected the means of making the water in a pump flow evenly in one direction, whether the plunger was on the upstroke or downstroke; and this flow meant the pump was very much more efficient. Here is a vignette of his mode of living at this time (1790). I take it from his son's life of his father published in 1872.

Mrs Dennis recollected Mr Trevithick at Ding Dong (mine) fixing his new plan of pumps there ... Her parents lived at Madron nearby and for two or three years Mr Trevithick came frequently to superintend the mine work, staying at their house a few days, or a week at a time.

He was a great favourite, full of fun and good humour, and a good story-teller. She had to be up at four in the morning to get Mr Trevithick's breakfast ready, and he never came to the house again until dark.

In the middle of the day a person came from the mines to fetch his dinner; he was never particular what it was. Sometimes when we were all sitting together talking, he would jump up, and before anyone had time to say a word, he was right away to the mine.

Henry Clark went to work in Dolcoath smith's ship in 1799. Captain Trevithick was putting in a plunger-pole lift; everybody said it would never answer, but the same lift is working there to this day (1869). Before this time they used buckets and pistons packed with gasket and a ring screwed on it; they used to jam with sand and gravel.

By now, Trevithick had met a man destined to be of enormous assistance to him. This was Davies Gilbert, that modest man of great intellect to whom Trevithick was to turn for theoretical help when working on some new mechanical development. Gilbert was an engineer, one of Britain's first experts, whose mastery of physics and the theories of engineering were of real national value at a time when the Government was facing problems created by the new climate of industry thrust upon them. Davies Gilbert became an MP and was chairman of many parliamentary committees on subjects varying from the building of trunk roads and harbours to advising practical engineers on theoretical problems and solving for them doubts pertaining, for example, to the degree to which use of the elasticity of steam could be put. Gilbert attained the great honour of being elected President of the Royal Society, as we have already heard.

Trevithick and he, two men from very different backgrounds – Trevithick, the intelligent earthy peasant, Gilbert the educated country landowner. Here is Gilbert's account of their first meeting. It is a letter written by Gilbert very much later, but giving an interesting picture of their relationship. It is written to J.S. Enys, Esquire, of Enys, near Truro:

I will give as good account as I can of Richard Trevithick. His father was the chief manager of Dolcoath Mine, and he bore the reputation of being the best informed and most skilful captain of all the mines ...

I knew the father very well, and about the year 1796 I remember hearing from Mr Jonathan Hornblower, that a tall and strong young man had made his appearance among engineers, and that on more than one occasion he had threatened some people who had contradicted him to throw them into the engineshaft. In the latter part of November of that year I was called to London as a witness in a steam-engine case between Messrs Boulton and Watt and Maberley. Then I believe that I first saw Richard Trevithick Junior, and certainly there I first became acquainted with him. Our correspondence commenced soon afterwards, and he was very frequently of the habit of calling at Tredrea to ask my opinion on various subjects that occurred to his mind – some of them very ingenious, and others so wild as not to rest on any foundation at all.

On one occasion Trevithick came to me and inquired with great eagerness as to what I apprehended would be the loss of power in working an engine by the force of steam raised to the pressure of several atmospheres, but instead of condensing, to let the steam escape into the air.

I, of course, answered at once that the loss of power would be one atmosphere, diminished power by the saving of an air pump with its friction, and in many cases with the raising of condensing water. I never saw a man more delighted; and I believe within a month several puffers were in actual work.

The lawsuit to which Gilbert refers was by the two well-known engineers, Boulton and Watt, whose mine engines were installed in many mines. They were northerners, who had a good machine when there was none other comparable. They were thus able to take advantage of this by including in the patents all manner of restrictions cleverly designed to forestall any future engineer being able to design improvements. This seriously curtailed, if not cut off, opportunities for other engineers to develop their own. A contemporary, one Mr Berenger, put it this way:

> Young engineers eager to win their spurs could hardly avoid infringing Watt's patent ... These unfortunate proceedings extended over several years and were at last decided in Watt's favour.
>
> Among much that was deplorable there was at least one good result, the steam-engine was fully discussed in open court and was expounded by the ablest of living men under the guidance of the acutest logicians. The driest detail acquired an emotional interest.
>
> If among the auditors there was genius awaiting ignition, there were sparks in abundance. It was here Trevithick was kindled ... he got ablaze with the vision of improvements which would follow the use of high-pressure steam.

I am not attempting in this essay on Trevithick the man, to go into technical detail, but it is necessary to understand the principle of Watts' mine engine that was the subject of the lawsuit. Today there are not many steam engines working, but up to thirty or forty years ago, most powerful engines, those in ships, on railways, mines and so on, were powered by steam at high pressure.

In Watts' time, mine engines used steam at *low* pressure. The low pressure steam slowly pushed up the piston to the top of the cylinder by being fed in from beneath. A jet of cold water was projected onto this which caused the steam to condense and drastically contract leaving a vacuum which provided the power to pull the piston down with enough power to work the pump. This was the power stroke of the engine. The steam was exhausted into the atmosphere and so the principle was very wasteful needing a prodigious amount of coal. It required, to be practical, a huge boiler in consequence.

It was the discovery of a way to control *high* pressure steam for action on both the top and under part of the piston, together with the need for only a moderate size boiler, that was to be Richard Trevithick's huge service to the mines of Cornwall, and, later, all over the world.

Watt, as can, perhaps, be understood, did not take at all kindly to the arrival of this new engine of young Trevithick, and did everything possible to persuade people the employment of high pressure steam was very dangerous, it being just not possible to construct a boiler strong enough that would not sooner or later burst with awful consequences. Indeed, in a letter to Davies Gilbert, Trevithick reported Watt as saying, 'You deserve hanging for bringing into use the high-pressure engine', but there was no turning back now. His improved cylindrical boiler was now trebling the work done by the Watt engines. By the turn of the century, Trevithick's engines saved the industry a coal bill of up to £100,000 per annum, and this at a time when Cornish mining interests were in a very depressed state.

This made it all the more difficult for Trevithick to develop his ideas for a steam carriage that would take passengers or freight. He spent some two years working on this, handicapped by the lack of money at this time of depression.

But he succeeded happily in another direction. He had married Jane Harvey shortly after his father died (1797). One of his friends, an engineer called William West, had before that become engaged to Johanna Harvey, sister of Henry Harvey of the famous Hayle Foundry, and it was that liaison that led to Trevithick's romance. Jane was tall, with fair hair and a brown complexion. They were a handsome couple, her husband, Capt'n Dick, as he was now called, being 6 foot 2 inches. Later in the marriage to this huge attractive genius of a man, Jane had occasion to draw on all the love and tolerance she could muster, as we shall see.

On their marriage, the couple lived in Redruth. For a time they had Watt for a near neighbour and, predictably, the two families were not on speaking terms.

William Murdoch, Watt's Scottish assistant, and the inventor of the gas lamp in 1792, also lived nearby. He used to mystify the miners (there are no coal mines, remember) by going about with a lighted lantern which he kept alight by coal-gas from a large bladder held under his arm.

This area around Redruth and Camborne was astonishingly rich in men of genius, each one of whose inventions were adopted all over the world in due course. Illogan spawned Trevithick, and I may be forgiven if I remind the reader, it also spawned the Tangye brothers whose contribution to engineering wonders I have related in *The Living Breath of Cornwall*.

An old account book of Trevithick's dated 1800, at the time of the building of the new steam carriage, gives details. His friend William West received pay for constructing models. Other mechanics worked in different mines repairing or improving boilers working the new high pressure engines. When they could be spared from the mines these men were working on the new steam-carriage. This was being put together in the smith's shop at Camborne [close to the Tyack hotel] having in it one small lathe and one or two smith's fires.

This was a more or less sporadic, and therefore lengthy, business, and it was not until Christmas Eve 1801 that the carriage was ready for its first trip with passengers.

The smith's shop was on the main London road along which the coach service operated. At that time of year in fact, only a van or covered waggon operated for the few who required to travel.

Northwards lay Lord de Dunstanville's mansion, Tehidy, where it was rather hilly. Southward, the road was a rude country lane in the worst possible condition, with a sharp curve at the beginning, and with steeper gradients than either of the two other roads.

Trevithick's son, Francis, tells of the greater difficulty of constructing an engine at that time in Cornwall than it was in his time thirty years later when he was working in the same shop in Harvey's of Hayle where William West had worked on the steam-carriage. Even then there were but a few hand lathes fixed on wooden benches, a few drilling machines and but one specialist lathe.

Francis Trevithick, in 1858, obtained the following reminiscence from an old man who had been working there with West.

In the year 1801, on Christmas Eve, coming on evening, Captain Dick got up steam, out in the high road, just outside the shop at Weith. When we see'd Captain Dick [Trevithick] was a-going to turn on steam, we jumped up, maybe seven or eight of us. 'Twas a stiffish hill going from the Weith up to Camborne Beacon, but she went off like a little bird.

When she had gone about a quarter of a mile, there was a roughish piece of road with loose stones; she didn't go quite so fast, and as it was a flood of rain and we were very squeezed together, I jumped off. She was going faster than I could walk, and went on up the hill about a quarter or half a mile further, when they turned her and came back again to the shop. Captain Dick tried her again next day: I was not there but heard someone say that some of the castings broke. Recollect seeing pieces of the engine in the ditch years afterwards, and suppose she ran against the hedge.

In the same year, Mr Newton, a resident in Camborne, informed Francis

> that he knew Mr Trevithick well and was to have been his
> pupil in engineering. He rode on the engine the first evening
> it was tried. It went half a mile up a steep hill and then
> returned to the workshop. The fire was blown by a double-
> acting bellows, worked by the engine. Was well acquainted
> with Murdoch and his friends in Cornwall, but never heard
> he had made a locomotive, or that Trevithick had been his
> pupil. The engine was called Captain Dick's puffer, from
> the steam and smoke puffing out of the chimney at each
> stroke of the engine.

As a matter of interest, the incline on Beacon Hill prevented horse-drawn vehicles from ascending at more than walking speed. It has been straightened long since.

Let us remember that we are recalling here the very first power-driven, passenger-carrying vehicle. Richard Trevithick, of Camborne, Cornwall, was the inventor of the first of all the countless road and rail engines that have served people since then and still do. For a long while it was the populist's impression that it was Stephenson to whom the honour for the rail locomotive belongs, but this is quite false and now accepted as such.

Trevithick's brother-in-law, Andrew Vivian, had helped in making parts for the steam-carriage in his own workshop and was present at the maiden run up Beacon Hill. He was an engineer, of a family who had some private means, so it was apparent to both that it would be a good idea to become partners, which they did a few days later over their Christmas dinner (1801).

They planned to build another vehicle for display in London but first had to sort out various problems up there; so off they went.

A letter written to Davies Gilbert after they had been away more than a fortnight gives a clear indication of the problems

that faced them. It is addressed to Mr Giddy who was in fact
Gilbert, who had changed his name for reasons connected
with a legacy:

No 1 Southampton St.,
Strand.
16 Jan 1802

Dear Mr Giddy,

Sir, – No doubt ere this you have been in expectation of
hearing from us: but so much time was taken up at Bristol
in contracting for engines, that we did not arrive here until
last Wednesday night.

We waited on Mr Sandys, who informed us that the
caveat had been secured and advised us to get the best
information we could of persons who were well acquainted
with patents and machines of what title to give the machine
and what was the intended use of it. The next day waited
on Mr Davy, and then Count Rumford to whom we had a
letter of introduction from Mr D. We found him a very
pleasant man and very conversant about fireplaces and the
action of steam for heating rooms, boiling water, dressing
meat etc; but did not appear to have studied much the
action of steam on pistons etc. The Count has given us a
rough draft of a fireplace which he thinks is best adapted for
our carriage, and Trevithick is now making a complete
drawing of it. We are to wait on the Count when the
drawing is completed and he has promised to give us all the
assistance in his power.

Mr Davy [this was Humphry Davy] says that a Mr
Nicholson, he thinks, will be a proper person to assist us in
taking out the patent, and we are to be introduced to him
tomorrow, and then shall immediately proceed with the
business. We shall not specify without your assistance, and
all our friends say that if we meet with any difficulty
nothing will be so necessary as your presence.

When we delivered Lord Dunstanville's letter to Mr
Graham he said he would give us everie assistance in his
power gratis if wanted.

Mr Pascoe Grenfell says he can find a way to the Attorney-General, if wanted.

It is strongly recommended to us to get a carriage made here and to exhibit it, which we also believe must be done.

Trevithick called on Mr Clayfield at Bristol, and is to call again on his return from Coalbrookdale to go in the mine. Mr Davy begins his lectures to the Royal Institution on Thursday next, and has given us tickets of admittance.

We remain in good health and spirits, Sir,

Your most obliged humble servants

R. Trevithick

A. Vivian.

Vivian had to return to Camborne, leaving Trevithick alone in London and making arrangements for the future appearance of a steam-carriage on view to the public and Government. Vivian wrote to his partner in a delightful way:

Camborne Feb 23rd, 1802

Dear Friend,

I arrived here last evening safe and sound, and missing my wife, was informed she was at your house where I immediately repaired. Your wife and little Nancy are very well but Richard is not quite well, having had a complaint which many children in the neighbourhood have been afflicted with; they are a little feverish when attacked, but it has soon worn off, as I expect your little son's will also; he is much better this morning and talked to me very cheerfully.

Mrs Trevithick is in pretty good spirits and requested I would not say a word to you of Richard's illness as she expected it to be soon over; but as I know you are not a woman, have given you an exact state of the facts. All my family, thank God, I found in perfect health, and all beg their kind remembrances to you, as does everyone I have met in the village.

'How do you do?' 'How is Captain Dick?' with the shake by the hand I have all this morning been employed.

In the Falmouth paper are the following lines: 'In addition to the many attempts to construct carriages to run without horses, a method has been lately tried in Camborne, in this county, that seems to promise success. A carriage has been constructed carrying a small steam engine, the force of which was found sufficient, upon trial, to impel the carriage containing several persons amounting at least to a ton and a half weight against a hill of considerable steepness, at the rate of 4 miles an hour; upon a level road it ran at eight or nine miles an hour. We have our information from an intelligent and respectable man who was in the carriage at the time, and who entertains a strong persuasion of the success of the project. The proprietors are now in London soliciting a patent to secure the property.

The same paper also mentions the increasing population of the parish of Camborne, viz. in one week nine women upraised, five pairs of banns published on Sunday, five more delivered to the clerk the following Saturday morning, eight children christened and five weddings.

Pray let me hear from you on receipt of this. When you go on with the York Water Company be sure to remember in the agreement that the new engine *is not to do more work than the old one unless paid in proportion.*

There is a postscript:

Mrs T (your beloved wife) begs her love, and expects to hear from you often.

Yrs etc. A. Vivian.

Three weeks later, Trevithick returned to Camborne to carry on with development and Vivian took his place in London to cope with the patent problems.

About the middle of 1802, a second more powerful engine had been built in Camborne and was sent to London in 1803. Andrew Vivian's account book makes it evident that this was sent to London by sea from Falmouth, for there are entries for quay dues in Falmouth and for carrying the engine to London in the name of the well-known shipping agents – still going strong – of Fox. Mr Felton, of Leather Lane, built the carriage in London, and this new steam-carriage, or locomotive, was a great improvement. It was not so heavy, and the design of a horizontal cylinder instead of the original vertical one (lowering the centre of gravity) greatly improved stability.

Another improvement was the chassis with larger wheels that could cope more easily with rough ground.

Trevithick, Andrew Vivian and William West were in London to make the first trip, and Arthur Woolf (later to become a famed engineer) who was by now in Trevithick's employ with the first high-pressure engine sent to London, came to watch.

Vivian drove it from Mr Felton's shop in Leather Lane, all the way to Lords Cricket Ground to Paddington, and home again by way of Islington, a journey of twenty miles through the busy streets of London.

At this time, Captain John Vivian was on his uncle's vessel in the London docks. While there he joined Trevithick on a run through London, taking 'the helm' himself. He recorded the fun on that day. They had started at four o'clock in the morning and went along Tottenham Court Road and City Road(?): there was a canal by the side of the road at one place, for he was thinking how deep it was if they should run into it. They kept going on for four or five miles, sometimes at the rate of nine miles an hour. 'I was steering,' he goes on, 'and Captain Trevithick and someone else were attending to the engine.

'Captain Dick came alongside of me and said, 'She's going all right!' 'Yes', I said, 'I think we had better go on to Cornwall.'

She was going along five or six miles an hour, and Captain Dick called out, 'Put the helm down, John!', and before I could tell what was up, Captain Dick's foot was upon the steering wheel handle, and we were tearing down six or seven yards of railing from a garden wall. A person put his head out from a window and called out, 'What the devil are you doing there! What the devil is that thing!'

They got her back to the coach factory under her own steam.

One last vignette of this sojourn in London. Francis Trevithick relates how, in 1860, he was told by a Mrs Humblestone that she remembered Mr Trevithick's steam-carriage going down Oxford Street: the shops were closed, and many people were waving handkerchiefs from the houses. No horses or carriages were allowed in the street during this event.

Trevithick now turned his attention to making 'a railroad' on which his locomotive could pull a load in a waggon or waggons. He, personally, had no finance to pay for development, but his enthusiasm, coupled to his obvious brilliance and charm enabled him to keep a number of plans developing at the same time. A major new figure came on the scene at this time in the person of Samuel Homfray, an ironmaster at Penydaren in South Wales. He had great expectations for Trevithick's high-pressure engines and he bought a share in their patent. He then made a bet with a Mr Hill, a neighbouring colleague, that he could make a steam locomotive to Trevithick's patents, that could pull ten tons of iron on the tramway (already in being for horse drawn vehicles) from Penydaren to Abercynon, a distance of nine and a half miles.

On 13th February 1804, the locomotive ran for the first time, and seven days later easily won the bet, though Mr Hill was to prove a poor loser and resisted payment.

Trevithick was heavily engaged at this time in supervising and erecting all manner of engines in places as far north as Newcastle, as well as London and Wales and elsewhere. Among these were the two Camborne and one London locomotive, an engine built at Coalbrookdale suitable for a railway, a Welsh tramroad engine and a Newcastle-on-Tyne railway engine.

In 1808, Trevithick constructed in London not only a

locomotive engine but also a special railway so that the London public might see the new high-pressure steam engine and see with their own eyes the superiority of the railway over the road for communication.

Here he is writing to Davies Gilbert about this London exhibit:

> About five days ago I tried the engine which worked exceedingly well; but the ground was very soft, and the engine (about 8 tons) sank the timber under the rails and broke a great number of them. I have now taken up the whole of the timber and iron ... we prove every part as we lay it down by running the engine over it by hand. I hope it will all be complete by the end of this week ...

In his account of this London venture, Francis Trevithick quotes this letter written about 1830 as being an interesting account by an engineer 'well known in his day':

> *Mr Trevithick's New Road Experiments in 1806* ... I think it is due to this extraordinary man to declare that about the year he laid down a circular railway in a field adjoining the New Road, near or at the spot now forming the southern half of Euston Square; that he placed a locomotive engine weighing about 10 tons on that railway – on which I rode with my watch in my hand – at the rate of 12 miles an hour, or more; that Mr Trevithick then gave his opinion that it would go 20 miles an hour or more on a straight railway; that the engine was exhibited at one shilling admittance, including a ride for the few who were not too timid; that it ran for some weeks, when a rail broke and occasioned the engine to fly off in a tangent and overturn, the ground being very soft at the time.

The engine must have gone off the rails literally 'at a tangent' for they were laid in a circle of about 40 yards diameter. This was enclosed in a high fence made of planks about 14 feet high so that only those who paid could see the action.

Unhappily not enough shillings rolled in to be able to keep the project going but it had done what was hoped for, that was that London had seen, and had had the opportunity to ride in, the very first railway, as it was later to be called.

Trevithick was now engaged in a totally different kind of problem; this was an attempt to make a tunnel under the Thames. He already had a finger in the Thames pie, for a dredger powered by one of his engines was working there successfully. He was also concerned about money and left it all to Andrew Vivian to worry about. So much was being expended yet (a feature well known to inventors) so impossible was it to get payment out of hard-headed business men.

The picture of this genius, far from his home, in a strange world of men with no other bent in life but to get money from others, invokes sympathy and pity: yet it would be wrong to do so for Trevithick was a man of optimism and supremely self-confident in his role of engineer/inventor. Even when hard-pressed, when experiments or sales or support from financial sources did not turn out as he would wish he was able to keep fighting for what he knew was right.

Fortunately, Trevithick was a good-tempered man and very simple, even frugal in his habits, and his wife, Jane, was nothing less than an angel. Jane added that he never gave trouble in 'home affairs', was satisfied with the most simple bed and board, and always busy with drawings and designs and experiments from early morning until bed-time. He was always quite confident they were all soon going to be rich, but did little or nothing (in the most charming way) to show concern for providing her with the bare necessities of life.

He was certainly delighted at the outcome of the circular railway, for the event confirmed for him his confidence in its possibilities. He immediately started thinking about something else.

An idea had come to him that iron plates might be used for making buoys for navigational and mooring purposes, and even ships. This, at the time, was to be ridiculed, for everyone knew that the only thing that floated was made of wood. He made designs of a number of alternatives which would have a working life far greater than anything of wood. He included tanks made of iron, particularly to hold drinking water in ships which until then had to rely on wooden tubs; even warships had no more secure way.

He put his scheme to the Admiralty who received it with indifference. Undismayed, and courageously determined, he went on with his plans for rolling iron plates and constructing iron ships, and machinery for loading and unloading, but always he was short of money.

Then he fell ill and fortune turned against him with a vengeance for he became bankrupt and was arrested for debt. How terrible it must have been, how lonely for this quite young man from Cornwall, far, far away from home and family, in a big heartless city. Everything was taken from him, valuable notes and diagrams which, in fact, were never returned to him. He was forced to lodge in a 'sponging house' in a street of refuge for debtors, and this was virtually imprisonment for there he had to stay until the debt was paid. 'A sponging house, I should tell you, was the place of preliminary confinement for debtors, and was kept by a bailiff or Sheriff's officer.

Prayers, however, were answered, and Jane suddenly felt he badly needed her. He had written many letters imploring her to come up to London and join him, but she never felt it was the truth for when in his company her place was way down on his list of priorities and she hardly saw him. Steam engines displaced her, and she felt that that hard fact and the tedious journey was not a prospect to face with relish. But now, she had felt the call. Reading again his imploring letters begging for her to come, she was left in no doubt. She would go, and as soon as possible. Four days by stage coach, with four children, one of them an infant in arms, and they were in London.

Jane found him very ill indeed; weak from typhus brought on by his sordid surroundings, delirious from anxiety and exhaustion from his superhuman efforts of the last few months. It is a pleasing picture for us to imagine his joyous disbelief when, lying in his cot in those squalid surroundings, despairing as to what the future held, he opened his eyes and found Jane there, Jane really there.

Not long after she arrived, while she was busying herself cleaning up the place and tidying it as best she could, she took his coat and emptied the bulging pockets. In one of them she had a moment's shock when she discovered her last two letters to him unopened. She looked down at him asleep, and felt betrayed by this disclosure, that he cared so little, that his calls for her to come and be with him were false. He was not asleep, but was watching her, incredulous that she was with him. A weak voice from the cot explained: he hadn't dared to open them lest her arguments against their reunion should have prevailed over his wishes.

With the help of a friendly doctor and the nursing by his loving wife he was slowly brought back to health; and news of a practical nature hastened the cure, for the reluctant sale of a patent brought enough money to clear his debt.

Trevithick, still a shadow of his former self, sailed for home in the *Falmouth Packet* in the manner previously mentioned. He took with him his eldest boy, while Jane and the others went by coach. It was thus, when he was still weak, that he learnt on reaching the house, his mother had, only just before, died.

However, his buoyant nature, now in its native environment, was not long in reasserting itself. His mind, teeming with ideas, his pockets empty of money, he nevertheless threw himself courageously into fostering developments that were imposed on him by his own inventions.

Though thousands of pounds had been lost in the previous five years, and all his mining property had gone, yet he carried on making himself responsible for the cost of constructing his machines, water-pressure engines, steam-pressure engines, iron tanks and wrought-iron boilers – and always everywhere in the air the power waiting to be created by his high-pressure steam-engines.

While we are on this list of his inventions, I feel it is the place to present to those still interested, a further detailing of other ventures that this remarkable Cornishman put in train; and I will put before you a catalogue of them that appeared in the Catalogue of the South Kensington Museum in 1884:

... Constructor of a tunnel beneath the Thames which he completed to within 100 feet of the proposed terminus and was then compelled to abandon the undertaking (nearly losing his life); inventor and constructor of steam-engines and machinery for the silver mines of Peru (capable of being transported in mountainous districts); also inventor and constructor of machinery for the Peruvian mint, and of furnaces for purifying silver ore; inventor of the screw propeller for ships, of floating docks, iron buoys, heating apartments, etc. Trevithick also found time for advising in the construction of the Plymouth breakwater and later advising the Dutch on the means for draining their marshes. This resulted in his having special chain-and-ball pumps for them, made at Hayle Foundry.

At the age of forty-five his life changed course to a most extraordinary degree and to an unexpected involvement.

On 20th October 1816, he sailed from Falmouth for South America, sure in his ever confident way that this time he was going to make a fortune. It was to come by supplying machinery to the Spaniards to re-open gold and silver mines that had been left to become flooded. He had made, the day before, a cheery farewell to his family, Jane marvelling, silently, at his incurable optimism, undiminished by the years of unmaterialised hope that lay behind. He was not to see her for eleven years.

The story of those eleven years on the other side of the world I leave for others to tell. They were years of both success and failure with Trevithick installing his engines under excruciating difficulties in a terrain of forests and mountains that had to be crossed with the only form of transport possible, namely pack animals. His practical abilities were stretched to the limit, but at the same time as he wrestled with the problems presented by the opening of old mines in outlandish places, his mind was alive with ideas, even to the extent of salvaging sunken ships.

Back home in Cornwall one year followed another for Jane who, far from enjoying fruits of a fortune, never once received any means of support during that long, long time.

Substantial allowance must be made to genius, whose feet are rarely on the ground and whose head is mostly in the air; but even Trevithick might have been expected to receive a lukewarm reception when at last he returned home. But no, such was the regard and affection he was held in that all were very glad to see him again, safe and sound, handsome and friendly as ever. This is how his son tells of his meeting with the father he did not know:

> In the early part of October 1827, I was then a boy at Bodmin school and was asked by the master if I had any particular news from home. Scarcely had the curiosity of the boys subsided, when a tall man with a broad-rimmed Leyhorn hat on his head entered at the door, and after a quick glance whereabouts, marched towards the master's desk at the other end of the room.
>
> When about half-way, and opposite my class, he stopped, took his hat off, and asked if his son, Francis, was there. Mr Boar, who had watched his approach, rose at the removal of his hat and replied in the affirmative.
>
> For a moment, a breathless silence reigned in school, while all eyes were turned on the gaunt, sun-burnt visitor; and the blood, without a defined reason, caused my heart to beat as though the unknown was his father, who eleven years before, carried him on his shoulder to the pier-head steps, and the boat going to the South Sea whaler.

Trevithick had nothing but the clothes he stood up in, a gold watch, a drawing compass, a magnetic compass, and a pair of silver spurs. His passage being unpaid, a chance friend enabled him to leave the ship; but he was naively of the opinion that in a month from that time he would be receiving £500,000 saved in the Cornish mines by the economies he had effected in their steam-engines.

Of course, he never received that fanciful sum, nor did he ever receive any recognition in cash or honours from the Government who were to gain so much from his inventions. Nevertheless, his resources of kindness, humility, and friendliness were, it seems, limitless. Disappointments, indifference by authority, poverty, failure, perhaps, as a father, never daunted his spirit which was as tall as his stature.

A month or so before his lonely death, he had written to his lifelong friend and adviser, Davies Gilbert. He concluded this letter with a defiant testament of his belief in himself and his inventions in the shadow of his financial circumstances.

It is a moment for me quietly to take leave of the subject of this memoir, and leave my reader alone to listen for the stifled cry of anguish from Richard Trevithick all those years ago, and to ponder on the raw set of muddled values that are set along the path that genius has to take:

I have been branded with folly and madness for attempting what the world calls impossibilities, and even from the great engineer, the late Mr James Watt, who said to an eminent scientific character still living [John Isaac Hawkins] that I deserved hanging for bringing into use the high-pressure engine. This so far has been my reward from the public.

But should this be all, I shall be satisfied by the great secret pleasure and laudable pride that I feel in my own breast from having been the instrument of bringing forward and maturing new principles and new arrangements of boundless value to my country.

However much I may be straightened in pecuniary circumstances, the great honour of being a useful subject can never be taken away from me, which to me far exceeds riches.

R.T.

IX

Endpiece and Lieutenant Goldsmith

Now, how, I wonder, am I going to be able to close this informal historical survey? Without being sentimental?

Spray and I have sailed together down and around the whole length of the Cornish coast and through the Cornish sea. And from our passage have emerged four volumes (Appendix G) of narrative in which readers are introduced to some fifty characters who have contributed to the Cornish story and earned a place in its tapestry. Well, I feel a good way to bid farewell is not to take ourselves too seriously. I intend, therefore, to end our voyage into Cornwall's past by introducing you to a man who, one hundred and fifty years ago, conducted an act of vandalism of a grand nature that no vandal today has yet approached. I use the word 'grand' advisedly for Lieutenant Goldsmith RN attracted a roar of protest such as today's Minister of Environment has never encountered; and grand, because, its nature and its motive and its perpetrator swung abuse round into smiles and cheers, from the same public, a few months later.

We are in Plymouth Sound now. Rame Head, that massive Cornwall cornerstone, is well astern. The tide is flooding, and *Spray*, with a rising breeze to her advantage, has her mainsail full, her big genoa bulging with this afternoon wind, a busy rippling wake astern of her as she makes good speed through rumpled water. Thus she flies, through the narrows of Drake's Island and the Hoe. Splendid sailing it is on the Hamoaze, the dockyard to starboard, its gracious Regency buildings white in the sun, and Mount Edgcumbe estate to port. Soon, in twenty minutes, we shall have picked up a mooring at Saltash, in the shadow of the great iron bridge, high above, of Brunel.

What a wonderful sail with which to end our voyage! What an apt place to moor under this monument to Victorian engineering. My eye fails to focus on the modern road bridge alongside it, fine in its own way as it is; but nor would I glance at a pebble alongside a diamond.

The Tamar river, on whose water we rest now, is the boundary between Cornwall and Devon. Its source is but a few hundred yards from the source of the marshland river which flows westward into the Atlantic. It makes, with the seas, Cornwall all but an island except for those few hundred yards.

Throughout its history Cornwall, in consequence of these natural boundaries, has been separate from the 'mainland', its culture, its industry, its commerce being independent and very much its own. Its people have rarely moved out of it, except by sea, until this wonderful bridge of Brunel, in 1859, spanned the river for his grand design, the Great Western Railway from London to Penzance. From then on Cornwall was no longer isolated, never the same again.

But look up there! Look up at the bridge with that train snaking along it – trains have been doing that on that bridge for *one hundred* and forty-five years and the structure is as safe as it was when first built.

The construction of it represented immense problems for Brunel. The Admiralty had insisted that it be 100 feet high above high water level so that naval vessels could pass under it. The two main spans suspended from those huge curved tubular girders that we can see from *Spray* now. Each of these is 465 feet long, and they were built on land, floated out on barges, and slowly notched up the concrete column, using each succeeding tide with ingenious skill to lift them.

Oh, my golly, that reminds me that it is Lieutenant Goldsmith that we are intending to meet. He brought upon himself a lifting problem of unusual kind, to be sure. Let us hear about it.

Davies Gilbert, that most distinguished President of the Royal Society who, as we have seen, was patron to both Sir Humphry Davy and Richard Trevithick, edited a parochial history of Cornwall, published in 1838. In it he included an account of the exploit of the young lieutenant. But before we visit the scene I must introduce it to you in the words of the incomparable antiquarian Dr William Borlase, writing eighty years before, in his *Antiquities of Cornwall*, second edition. He says:

> In the parish of St. Levan, there is a promontory called Castle Trerin. This cape consists of three distinct groups of rocks.
>
> On the western side of the middle group, near the top, lies a large stone, so evenly poised, that any hand may move it to and fro; but the extremities of its base are at such a distance from each other, and so well secured by their nearness to the stone which it stretches itself upon that it is morally impossible that any lever, or indeed, force (however applied in a mechanical way) can remove it from its present situation.

Well, such an assertion was a tantalising challenge to be disproved by anyone dull-witted enough not to equate bravado with vandalism. The latter we are troubled by today as we well know; our forbears had to bear it, too, as, perhaps, we didn't all know.

I leave Davies Gilbert to tell you the story of the Logan Rock. We pick it up when a naval cutter from Plymouth was on a cruise along the coast from Land's End. She was on the look-out for smugglers landing their contraband on shore.

Lieutenant Goldsmith – incidentally nephew of Oliver Goldsmith, the celebrated novelist and poet – was in charge, and it must have been off Porthcurno that he and his crew of twelve seamen, cooked up this idea of showing they could do the impossible by knocking down the famed Logan Rock.

At all events:

> On this eighth of April they left their boat beached in a small cove, climbed up the cliff, and then higher to the place where

this 90 ton stone was balancing. By a continued application of their united strength they threw this huge mass into vibrations of such extent as to cause the convex surface at last to slide from its horizontal base, most fortunately in the direction opposite to that in which they stood. The rock was saved from falling to the ground, and from hence probably into the sea, by a narrow chasm which caught it in the descent.

Mr Goldsmith, having thus achieved what had been declared impossible by the highest authority that Cornwall could produce, must have congratulated himself on such complete success; but the sensations of all the neighbourhood were entirely at variance from those of the gallant officer; fears were even entertained for his life. What he had done excited the greatest indignation in Penzance as it did in every part of Cornwall and throughout the kingdom, not least because it rendered two poor families bereft of an income they gleaned from visitors.

A meeting of the Magistrates and principal persons was contemplated for the purpose of representing the affair to Government, but the Editor of this work being then in London, and having the honour of being known to all the Lords of the Admiralty, he went there, and representing the exploit that had been performed in the light of an indiscreet frolic, he proposed that the Admiralty should lend a proper apparatus, and send it from Plymouth, while he on his part would endeavour to raise an adequate sum of money; and that Lieut. Goldsmith, having thrown down this natural curiosity, should superintend the putting up of it again. The terms were accepted, and thirteen capstans with blocks, chains, etc, were sent from the dockyard.

The Editor, having commenced a contribution of money with twenty-five pounds, raised it to a hundred and fifty. On the 2 November, in the presence of thousands, amidst ladies waving their handkerchiefs, men firing *feux-de-joye*, and universal shouts, Mr Goldsmith had the satisfaction and the glory of replacing this immense rock in its natural position, uninjured in its discriminating properties. In consequence of the Editor making a second application to the Admiralty, and of his commencing another contribution of money with five pounds, Lanyon Cromlech was also replaced by the same apparatus.

*

And now back to *Spray*.

'Ahoy there! Anyone aboard?' The voice was friendly but authoritative. I pulled myself up from the bunk where I'd been resting down below and put my head through the hatch. The young face above the gunwhale belonged to Customs.

'Anything to declare, sir?'

'No, Officer. We've been in home waters.'

'Your home port?'

'Falmouth.'

'Where are you bound for, now?'

'Well, I hadn't really thought. Not abroad anyway.'

For a minute or so I watched his rubber dinghy bouncing downstream – a tiny dot, prominent only because of the buzz of the fussy little engine.

'Where are you bound for?' That's what he had asked.

Well, with three score years and ten well behind me I qualify for the end of the voyage being just over the horizon. And when, finally, I reach it, I warrant I will hear the poet's song that he wrote for the widow of Admiral Boscawen, the forbear of the Lords of Falmouth, of Tregothnan:

> Why mourn the dead? You wrong the grave
> From storms that safe resort;
> We still are tossing out at sea
> Our Admiral's in port.

Appendix A

Pertaining to Chapter II

Dr Borlase on the Rise and Fall of Families (*see* Lysons p. lxxxvi)

'It is a melancholy reflection to look back on so many great families as have formerly adorned the County of Cornwall, and are now no more; the Grenvilles, the Arundells, Carminows, Champernons, Bodrugans, Mohuns, Killigrews, Bevilles, Trevanions, which had great sway and possessions in these parts.

'The most lasting families have only their seasons, more or less, of a certain constitutional strength. They have their spring, their summer sunshine glare, their wane, decline, and death; they flourish and shine perhaps for ages; at last they sicken, their light grows pale, and, at crisis when the offsets are withered, and the old stock is blasted, the whole tribe disappears, and leaves the world as they have done Cornwall.

'There are limits ordained for everything under the sun. *Man will not abide in honour*. Of all human vanities family-pride is one of the weakest.

'Reader, go thy way; secure thy name in the book of life, where the page fades not, nor the title alters nor expires: leave the rest to Heralds and the Parish Register.'

Appendix B

Sir Humphry Davy: A short list from his papers read before the Science Establishment, and indicating the breadth of his experiments and vision.

1. 'An Account of some Galvanic Combinations formed by single metallic plates and fluids.' *Read 18th June 1801.*
2. 'Experiments and Observations on certain Astringent Vegetables, and their operation in Tanning.' *24th February 1803.*
3. 'On a method of analysing stones containing a fixed alkali, by means of Boracic Acid.' *16th May 1805.*
4. 'On some new Phenomena of Chemical Changes produced by Electricity.' *19th November 1807.*
5. 'Electro-chemical Researches on the Decomposition of the Earths, with north Observations on the Metals obtained from the Alkaline Earths.' *30th June 1808.*
6. 'An account of some new Researches on the nature of Alkalis, Phosphorus, Sulphur, Carbonaceous matter, and the Acids hitherto compounded.' *15th December 1808.*
7. 'Researches on the Oxy-muriatic Acid, its nature and combinations, and experiments on Sulphur and Phosphorous made in the laboratory of the Royal Institution.' *12th July 1810.*
8. 'On a new detonating compound.' *5th November 1812.*
9. 'An Account of some new Experiments on the Fluoric Compounds and other objects of Chemical Enquiry.' *13th February 1814.*
10. 'Some Experiments on a new Substance which becomes a

Violet-coloured Gas by heat.' *20th January 1814*.
11. 'Some Experiments and observations on the Colours used in Painting by the Ancients.' *23rd February 1815*.
12. 'Some Experiments on the combustion of the Diamond.' *23rd June 1814*.
13. 'Some Researches on Flame.' *25th January 1816*.
14. 'Some Observations on the formation of Mists in particular situations.'
15. 'On the Magnetic Phenomenon produced by Electricity.' *16th November 1820*.
16. 'Further Researches on the Magnetic Phenomenon produced by Electricity, with some new Experiments on the properties of Electrified bodies in their relations to conducting Powers and Temperature.'
17. 'On the Application of Liquids formed by the condensation of Gases as mechanical Agents.' *17th April 1823*.
18. 'On the corrosion of Copper Sheathing by seawater; and on methods of preventing this effect, and on their application to ships of war.' *24th June 1824*.
19. 'On the Phenomena of Volcanoes.'

His publications are:
1. *Experimental Essays on Heat, Light, and on the Combinations of Light, with a new theory of Respiration*, 1799.
2. *Researches Chemical and Philosophical, chiefly concerning Nitrous Oxide and its Respiration*, 1800.
3. *A Syllabus of a Course of Lectures*.
4. *An Introductory Lecture*, 1801
5. *Elements of Chemical Philosophy*, 1812.
6. *Elements of Agricultural Chemistry*, 1813.
7. *On the Safety Lamp for Coal Miners; with some Researches on Flame*, 1818.
8. *Salmonia; or Days of Fly-Fishing*.
9. *Consolations in Travel; or the Last Days of a Philosopher*.

Appendix C

Pertaining to Chapter V

Eye-witness account of action at sea – Trafalgar, 1805.

'...I was looking out of the bowport at the moment that a shot struck our ship on the stern between wind and water. It was the first time I had ever seen the effect of a heavy shot; it made a great splash, and, to me, as I then thought, a very unusual noise, throwing a great deal of water in my face. I very naturally started back, as I believe many a brave fellow has done. Two of the seamen quartered at my guns, laughed at me. I felt ashamed, and resolved to show no more such weakness.

'This shot was very soon succeeded by some others not quite so harmless: one came into the bowport, and killed the two men who had witnessed my trepidation. My pride having been hurt that these men should have seen me flinch, I will own that I was secretly pleased when I saw them removed beyond the reach of human interrogation.

'It would be difficult to describe my feelings on this occasion. Not six weeks before, I was the robber of hen-roosts and gardens – the hero of a horse-pond, ducking an usher – now suddenly, and almost without any previous warning or reflection, placed in the midst of carnage, and an actor in one of those grand events by which the fate of the civilized world was to be decided.

'A quickened circulation of blood, a fear of immediate death, and a still greater fear of shame, forced me to an involuntary and frequent change of position; and it required some time, and the best powers of intellect, to reason myself into that frame of mind in which I could feel as safe and as unconcerned as if we had been in harbour. To this state I at last did attain, and soon felt ashamed of the perturbation under which I laboured before the firing began. I prayed, it is true; but my prayer was not that of faith, or trust, or of hope – I prayed only for safety from imminent personal danger; and my orisons consisted of one or two short, pious ejaculations, without a thought of repentance for the past or amendment for the future.

'But when we had once got fairly into action, I felt no more of this, and beheld a poor creature cut in two by a shot with the same indifference that at any other time I should have seen a butcher kill an ox. Whether my heart was bad or not, I cannot say; but I certainly felt my curiosity was gratified more than my feelings shocked, when a raking-shot killed seven, and wounded three more. I was sorry for the men, and, for the world, would not have injured them; but I had a philosophic turn of mind; I like to judge of causes and effects; and I was secretly pleased at seeing the effect of a raking-shot' – FRANK MILDMAY.

Appendix D

Pertaining to Chapter V

Copy of a letter from the widow of Captain Millon of the *Cleopatra*, to Sir Edward Pellew (later, Lord Exmouth). *Translation.*

Rochefort-sur-Mer
31 July, 1793

Sir,

I have received the two letters which you have had the complacence to write to me. The afflicting news of the death of my dear husband, which they brought me, is to me a thunderstroke. Nothing can console me for so great a loss as he was the only resource of myself and my five children, and with him our only hope is lost.

I always feared, and with reason, that he would find his death in his courage and activity in the service of his Country.

It remains, however, for me to thank you for your generosity, which I took care should be publicly known, as I sent a copy of your letter to the Minister. When you do me the favour to send me the effects belonging to my husband (and which at this moment form a great part of my fortune) I beg that in addition to that generosity, these effects, as well as all the papers relative to his equipment or otherwise, may be forwarded as soon as possible; and to the end that I may get them without risk, that they be accompanied by a passport, which will undoubtedly be granted on your application.

The part you have already taken in what is so interesting to me assures me that you will use all possible means farther to oblige me, and for which in addition to my obligations, I thank you beforehand.

If you have been at any expense on account of my husband be

pleased to keep as much of his effects in your hands as will repay you: otherwise, if you will let me know the sum, I will be exact in remitting you the amount...

Pray, sir, do me the further service to apprise me with the time of departure of my husband's effects, the name of the vessel and commander and the place of destination, that I might write to someone to receive them.

The safest way, in my apprehension (if you should not find an opportunity to forward them to Rochefort) would be to direct them to the Commandant of the Marine at the first port that they arrive at: the passport securing them on their passage to Rochefort, their ultimate destination.

I rely on your goodness
And am, Sir
Your affectionate Nance . Millon.

[N.B.   *It should be remembered, while reading the foregoing, that it refers to an action that had taken place only six weeks before, and that hostilities between France and England were still in progress.*]

Appendix E

Pertaining to Chapter VII

The Journey to London.

Travel facilities were raw and tiring. The journey by post-chaise to London took a week. Though I have no details of Opie's and Wolcot's journey, we have details of route and time and stops of Mrs Falck, of Falmouth in 1794, as recorded in her Journal:

'August 28th. Set off from Falmouth for London. Din'd at St. Austell. Drank tea at Lostwithiel. Slept at Liskeard.

'29th. Call'd at Catchfrench. Din'd at Plymouth. Drank tea at Ivebridge. Slept at Ashburton.

'30th. Slept at Chudleigh. Reached Exeter by one. Din'd at Cullompton, changed horses at Wellington and Taunton. Reached Bridgewater where we slept.

'31st. Breakfasted at B. Changed at Glastonbury. Rode through Wells, din'd at Old Downs (?) Inn. Chang'd at Chippenham and reach'd Marlborough to supper, when we slept. Drank tea at Bath.

Sept. 1st. Breakfasted at Speenhill. Din'd at Maidenhead Bridge. Chang'd horses at Hounslow, got to London at ten.

2nd. Very much fatigu'd. Lay abed best part of the day.'

In Susan Gay's *Old Falmouth* she writes of the mail coach service to London in the early 1800's. As we have seen, it took nearly a week a few years earlier; and potential hazards were such that passengers were accustomed to make their wills before setting off.

The fare was about six pounds and the journey took some

sixty hours, subsequently reduced to less than fifty. Bristol and Exeter were the stopping places for the night, and four to six horses were used, galloping all the way. The horses were changed every ten miles.

There was a cheaper service called Russell's Wagons. This was primarily a goods service but passengers were taken, and they slept on straw. The journey took eleven days.

Appendix F

Pertaining to Chapter VII

Borough Electoral Corruption

During the seventeenth century and up until 1832, there were two County Members of Parliament (as opposed to town or hamlet). In his pamphlet *'When Cornwall had 44 MPs'*, A.C. Glubb relates the way huge sums were spent at each County Election, the Poll being open several days.

Public houses gave free drinks all over the County, and at one County Election the liquor consumed at the old *Red Lion* in Truro, and paid for by one candidate, would have more than filled its extensive cellars. £20,000 was not an excessive sum for a Candidate to spend.

Cornwall was the most represented County in Parliament in the United Kingdom. There were 44 Members [there are five today], one less than the whole of Scotland. Looe had as many Members as the City of London (4).

Appendix G

And now Adieu

The three previous volumes of the four that go to make up my informal historical survey of notable goings-on by Cornwall's men and women, are:

Voyage into Cornwall's Past (1979)

The Living Breath of Cornwall (1980)

Cornwall and the Tumbling Sea (1981)

and lastly this final one,

Proud Seas and Cornwall's Past (1982)

> So, Readers,
> My Friends,
> Adieu!
> Adieu!

Bibliography

Memoirs of the Life of Sir Humphry Davy, by his brother, John, 2 vols, Longman, London, 1837

The Life of Sir Humphry Davy, 2 vols, J.A. Paris, Colburn & Bentley, London, 1831

Cornish Worthies, W.H. Tregellas, Elliot Stock, London, 1884

Famous Men and Women of Cornish Birth, I.D. Spreadbury, Kingston. Mevagissey, 1972

Bibliotheca Cornubiensis, Courteney and Boase, vol. i and ii, London, 1878

Researches, Chemical and Philosophical, H. Davy, J. Johnson, London, 1800

Scenes and Adventures in the Life of Frank Mildmay, London, 1805

The British Seaman, Christopher Lloyd, Collins, London, 1968

Problems of Medecine at Sea, Monograph No.12, National Maritime Museum, 1974

Voyages and Discoveries of the British Nation, 1552–1616, Richard Hakluyt, ed. Richard Irving, Heinemann, London, 1927

The Navy of Britain, Michael Lewis, Allen and Unwin, London, 1948

Life of Admiral Viscount Exmouth, Edward Osler, Smith Elder Cornhill, London, 1835

Samuel Kelly, 18th Century Seaman, ed. Crosbie Garstin, Jonathan Cape, London, 1925

Girdle Round the World, Hugh Barty-King, Heinemann, London, 1980

History of Cornwall, Richard Polwhele, Cadell and Davies, London, 1803

Shipwreck Investigated, Henry Trengrouse, James Truthan, Falmouth, 1817

Reminiscences, Richard Polwhele, vol i, Nicholson, London, 1836

When Cornwall had 44 MPs, A. de C. Glubb, A.C. Jordan, Truro, 1814

Wreck and Rescue Around the Cornish Coast, Noall and Farr, Bradford Barton, Truro, 1965

Opie and his Works, Jope Rogers, J.A.

Opie, John – Memoir, Peter (Mr), R.I.C. Journal, Truro, 1953

Memorials of Amelia Opie, Miss Brightwell

Opie, John and his Circle, Hutchinson & Co., London, 1911

A Cornish Giant, Edith Harper, Spon, London, 1913

Dictionary of National Biography, Oxford University Press

Life of Trevithick, Francis Trevithick, 2 vols., Spon, London, 1872

Voyage from England to India, Edward Ives, London, 1773

The Harveys of Hayle, Edmund Vale, D. Bradford Barton, Truro, 1966

Beyond the Blaze, A.C. Todd, D. Bradford Barton, Truro, 1967

The Cornish Beam Engine, D.B. Barton, D. Bradford Barton, Truro, 1965

Richard Trevithick, James Hodge, Shire Publications, Aylesbury, 1973

Brunel's Ships, Dumpleton and Miller, Uffington Press, Melksham, 1975

Parochial History of Cornwall, Davies Gilbert, Nichols and Son, Oxford, 1838

England's Riviera, Stone, Kegan Paul, Trench, Trubner, London, 1923

The Cornish Coast, Charles Harper, Chapman and Hall, London, 1910

The King's England: Cornwall, Arthur Mee, Hodder and Stoughton, London, 1937

Old Falmouth, Susan Gay, Headley Bros., London, 1903

Post Office Packet Service, History of, A.H. Norway, Macmillan, London, 1895

Sailing Packets to West Indies, L.E. Britnore, British W. Indies Study Circle, No.5, 1973

Around the Fal, Fal History Group, University of Exeter, 1980

Story of Flushing, Ursula Redwood, Author, 1967

James Silk Buckingham, autobiography, Longman, London, 1855

British Channel Pilot, Hobbs and Wilson, London, 1859, re-published Barton, Truro, 1972

Cornish Characters and Strange Events, S. Baring-Gould, Bodley Head, London, 1909

Lysons Magna Britannica, vol. iii, Cadell and Davies, London, 1814

Lake's Parochial History of Cornwall, vols i and iv, Truro, 1867, 1872

History of Cornwall, Polwhele, vols i, ii and iii, Cadell and Davies, Falmouth, 1803

Natural History of Cornwall, William Borlase, Oxford, 1758

History of Cornwall, Drew, vol. ii, Helston, 1824

Naval Side of British History, Callender, London, 1924

Opie (John) Biographical Note on, RIC Journal xvi, Truro

Royal Cornwall Gazette, 1801 *et seq.*

West Briton, 1810 *et seq.*

London Gazette Extraordinary, 6th Nov, 1805

Journal of the Society of Nautical Research, vol xxiv, 1938

Index